ANGLO-DUTCH LINKS 1560-1860

By
David Dobson

Copyright © 2020
by David Dobson
All Rights Reserved

ISBN 9780806359069

INTRODUCTION

Social and economic links between the Netherlands and England have existed from the medieval period. During the early modern period, from the Reformation onwards, these links intensified when the two countries united in opposing a common enemy in the shape of Spain, then part of the Hapsburg Empire. At other times economic rivalry led to war between England and the United Provinces. The Reformation of the early sixteenth century led to the division of the Netherlands into the Catholic Spanish Netherlands, roughly today's Belgium, and the Calvinist Seven United Provinces of the northern Netherlands. The Seven Provinces were Holland, Zeeland, Utrecht, Friesland, Groningen, Overijssel, and Gelderland, with Drenthe associated. The Spanish Netherlands included Flanders, Brabant, and Limburg. From 1568 to 1648 the Dutch fought the Spanish in The Eighty Years War, to establish and maintain their independence, during which time the English provided them with substantial military support. In the aftermath the port of Antwerp, which previously had been the major entrepot in northern Europe, was replaced by Rotterdam.

The rise of the Dutch United East India Company and the Dutch West India Company, supported by the Dutch merchant navy, enabled the Dutch to establish an empire in America, the Caribbean, Africa, and Asia. Since England was simultaneously expanding its merchant fleet and empire, rivalry and conflict between the two broke out in Europe and America. The English Navigation Acts, from 1651, were aimed at reducing the power of the Dutch merchant marine, which had been the leading sea-power in western Europe, by restricting colonial trade to English shipping.

In the sixteenth and seventeenth centuries, religious refugees settled both in the Netherlands and England: English Puritans ventured to Holland, for example in Leiden; and Calvinists from Flanders, Zealand and Holland, emigrated to England, establishing the Dutch Reformed churches in London.

Throughout the period trading links between the two countries were expanded leading to merchants and craftsmen settling in ports such as London, Rotterdam, and Antwerp. The establishment of universities in the Netherlands, especially Leiden's medical school, attracted students from England during the period.

This book attempts to identify English people in the Netherlands, temporarily or permanently, and similarly Dutch or Flemish people in England. It also lists people trading between the two countries, as named in domestic records as well as in colonial records.

Throughout the volume, readers will encounter the terms *denization* and *naturalization,* which require some explanation. Letters of denization were official government grants allowing persons born abroad to be treated as if they had been born in England. The English Crown first started issuing them in the 1370s, in response to the desire of some wealthier immigrants to have a reasonably full range of legal rights. Recipients were required to renounce their former loyalties and take an oath of allegiance to the King of England. In return, they were to be treated in roughly the same way as any English subject born within the realm. They and their descendants were entitled to own land, property and other possessions in England and to have their legal cases dealt with in English courts.

Denization was somewhat different from the later process of naturalization, which became available in the sixteenth century. Denization allowed many rights, but it did not necessarily exclude people from paying customs duties (on exports, as well as imports) at the higher rate normally charged to foreigners. Nor did denization necessarily allow the recipient to participate in parliamentary elections; it was only naturalization that later explicitly allowed that right.

David Dobson
Dundee, Scotland, 2020

ANGLO-DUTCH LINKS, 1560-1860

REFERENCES

ARM   Madeira Regional Archives

Acts PCCol   Acts of the Privy Council, Colonial

BM   British Museum

Cal. HO.pp   Calendar of Home Office papers

CLRO   City of London Record Office

F   Fastii Ecclesiae Scoticanae, Edinburgh

GM   Gentleman's Magazine, series

HBRS   Hudson's Bay Record Society

NEHGS   New England Historic Genealogy Society

NLS   National Library of Scotland

NRS   National Records of Scotland

PCC   Prerogative Court of Canterbury

RNA   Rotterdam Notorial Archives

SPDom   Calendar of State Papers, Domestic

SP.Foreign   Calendar of State Papers, Foreign

TNA   The National Archives, Kew

TNT   Trinity House Transactions

ANGLO-DUTCH LINKS, 1560-1860

ABEELES, JOHN, son of Nicholas Abeeles of Roussalaer, Flanders, a citizen of Kortrijk, and a member of the Dutch congregation in London, probate, 1610, PCC

ABEELES, WILLIAM, born in Roussalaer, Flanders, a citizen of Kortrijk, and a member of the Dutch congregation in London, later in Haarlem, probate, 1612, PCC

ABEELS, WILLIAM, born in Haarlem, settled in London, Probate, 1629, PCC

ABERS, MARIA, was granted a pass to go to Holland on 24 April 1690. [SPDom.1690.565]

ABERSON, FREDERIK ALEXANDER, from the Netherlands, was naturalised in England on 24 September 1866. [TNA.HO.1.98.3359]

ABRAHAMS, JACOB, a Dutch carpenter imprisoned in the Tower of London, bound for the shipyard at Chatham, Kent, in November 1670. [SPDom.1670.518]

ADAM, JOHN, from Hainault in the Netherlands, residing in the City of London, probate, 1571, PCC

ADAMS, EDMUND, master of the Peter of Boston, from Boston bound for Rotterdam on 10 November 1634, arrived in Boston, Lincs., on 20 December 1634 from Rotterdam. [TNA.E190.393.1]

ADAMS, JOSEPH, master of the Unity of Boston, arrived in Boston, Lincs., on 17 January 1634 from Amsterdam. [TNA.E190.396.1]

ADAMSON, RICHARD, a servant from London, in Brussels, probate, 1690, PCC

ANGLO-DUTCH LINKS, 1560-1860

ADRIAN, GILES, master of the Bonadventure of Flushing, [Vlissingen] arrived in London on 3 December 1567 from Flushing. [TNA.E190.4.2]

ADRIANSON, ANDREW, master of the Cock of Antwerp [Antwerpen], arrived in London on 3 December 1567. [TNA.E190.4.2]

ADRIANSON, JOHN, CORNELIS JACOBWITSON, WILLEM ISBRANDSON, and others of Amsterdam, were granted a commission for the restoration of their ship Red Fish of Elpindam and its cargo, loaded at St Michael's and captured by the Diamond of Bridgewater and the Bank Clovell of Bristol and taken there, August 1592. [SP.Foreign iv.100]

ADRYASON, LEONARD, from Flanders, a grant of denization in England, 26 May 1568. [HRS.7.72]

ADRIANSON, CORNELIS, master of the Angel of Bergen-op-Zoom arrived in London on 25 November 1567. [TNA.E190.4.2]

ADRIANSON, PAUL, master of the Mary Magdalene of Middelburg also Francis Hauck were to be restituted for cargo taken by Captain Thomas Favell, September 1593. [SPForeign.iv.100]

AERTSS, alias CUTTING, ANNE, daughter of Jasper Aertss, widow of William Cutting, born in Welde near Turnhoute, The Hague, [Den Haag] of the Dutch Church in London, probate, 1608, PCC

AANTEN, BARTOLOMEW, a mariner from Holland, resident in St Catherine's parish, Middlesex, aboard the Sceptre bound for the East Indies, died in the ship Tiger, probate 1698, PCC

ANGLO-DUTCH LINKS, 1560-1860

ALARDSON, SIMON, master of the Falcon of Amsterdam in London on 6 October 1567; arrived in London on 8 November 1567 from Amsterdam. [TNA.E190.4.2]

ALBERTSON, CORNELIUS, of Medemblik, master of The Angel, was commissioned to recover his ship and its cargo of cotton wool, captured by the Eleanor of London and taken to Hampton, November 1590. [SPForeign.iv.99]

ALBINES, BERNARD, in Demerara, 1779, see Robert Elliot's will dated May 1779. [NRS.RD4.235.748]

ALBRIGHT, CORNELIS, master of the Fortune of Bruges arrived in London on 19 November 1567 from Bruges. [Brugge] [TNA.E190.4.2]

ALLERTSON, ALERT, master of the Pelican of Amsterdam arrived in London on 12 November 1567 from Amsterdam. [TNA.E190.4.2]

ALLERTON, ISAAC, born 1586, a tailor from London, with his first wife Mary, born 1588, died 1621, and children, Bartholomew born 1612, Remember born 1614, and Mary born 1616, from Leiden aboard the Speedwell and later the Mayflower bound for America in 1620

AMYRAUT, PAUL, born in Germany, army chaplain at Breda, minister to the Reformed Church in Utrecht from 1637-1638, vicar of East Deerham, Norfolk, in 1648, rector of Mundesley in 1660. [F.7.554]

ANCION, ISODORE JOSEPH, from Belgium, was naturalised in England on 30 April 1870. [TNA.HO1.163.6510]

ANDREWES, JOHN, a Dutchman, voluntarily on board the Conquer bound from London for Virginia on 14 August 1657. [TNA.CO1.13.29]

ANKMAN, ANTHONY, merchant of Middelburg, to be compensated for cargo taken by Captain Knight of the Saucy Jack of Hampton from aboard the Bonadventure of Roscoff, in April 1589. [Cal.SPForeign.iv.99]

APPELMAN, BATHASAR, former burgomaster of Amsterdam, co-owner of The Jonas of Amsterdam was captured on way home from Barbary and taken to England in 1591. [SPForeign.84.xliv]

ARIENTIE, …., a Dutchwoman with children, was granted a pass to go to Holland on 25 April 1690. [SPDom.1690.566]

ARNOOT, CHARLES, from Belgium, was naturalised in England on 19 July 1854. [TNA.HO1.56.1843]

ASCHER, JOSEPH, from the Netherlands, was naturalised in England on 12 March 1864. [TNA.HO.1.113.4310]

AUDLEY, THOMAS, of St Mary Magdalen, London, in Antwerp, [Antwerpen], probate 1578, PCC

BACK, PETER, born in Brussels, a merchant in London, probate, 1570, PCC

BACKWELL, EDWARD, a citizen and alderman of London, died in the Hague, [Den Haag], probate, 1698, PCC

BAILLIE, JAMES, formerly a merchant on St Eustatia, died in Ealing on 7 September 1793. [GM.63.869]

BAILLIE, RALPH, a merchant in Amsterdam, trading with Boston, Lincolnshire, in 1617. [TNA.E190. 394.15]

ANGLO-DUTCH LINKS, 1560-1860

BALDWIN, MARY, from Quinoborome, Leicestershire, a widow, died in Bruges, [Brugge] Flanders, probate 1685, PCC

BALLE, DAVID, born 15 November 1692, Member of the Council of Demerara, died 8 November 1734. [Coomacha Plantation gravestone, Demerara] 'Hier levt begraven de Heer David toberBalle, raaten mester planter op de plantagie en Markay; is geboernen der 15 Nov. 1692, en gerlonee de 8 Nov. 1734'.

BALLE, LORANCE, master of the Sea Rider of Amsterdam arrived in London on 8 October 1567. [TNA.E190.4.2]

BALLETT, THOMAS, a gentleman of Westminster and of Flanders, probate, 1692, PCC

BANNISTER, JAMES, born 1624, Governor of Surinam, died 10 November 1674. [St Catherine's gravestone, Jamaica]

BARRELL, THEODORE, a merchant in Grenada and in St Eustatius, husband of Mary Barrell, a memorial, 1790. [TNA.AO13.137.4]

BART, GARET, master of the Ships Coy of Amsterdam arrived in London on 18 November 1567 from Amsterdam. [TNA.E190.4.2]

BARTOLFF, MICHAEL, born in Comen, Flanders, in Colchester, Essex, probate. 1627, PCC

BARTON, GEORGE, born 1596, from Wollerbe, Lincolnshire, licensed to go to Holland in 1637. [TNA]

BARUCHSON, ARNOLD DE BEER, from the Netherlands, was naturalised in England. [TNA.HO.1.17.29]

ANGLO-DUTCH LINKS, 1560-1860

BAUWINS, FRANCIS, master of the Spliedegle of Bruges arrived in London on 20 October 1567 from Bruges. [Brugge] [TNA.E190.4.2]

BEAUCHAMP, JOHN, a merchant from London, son of John Beauchamp in Northamptonshire, will subscribed in Amsterdam, probate, 1615, PCC

BELLORE, MARINUS, a seaman from Flushing, [Vlissingen], was granted denization in Ireland on 6 September 1671. [BM.Egerton.1720]

BENGALL, ADRIAN, a master mariner from Middelburg in Zealand, was granted denization in Ireland on 16 November 1671. [BM.Egerton.1720]

BENNET, RICHARDSON, an Englishman, rented a house next to Huiszittenhuis in Rotterdam, to Jeronimo Henriques Serra, on 22 April 1618. [RNA.611.390]

BENTINCK, Count WILLIAM, President of the States General of Holland, correspondence with Gedney Clarke, re Demerara and Berbice, 1762-1766. [BM. Egerton.1720]

BERGNER, KARIL WILLEM EDZARD, from the Netherlands, was naturalised in England on 2 May 1862. [TNA.HO.1.15.3821]

BERWARD, HENRY, born in Tilleur in Liege, [Luik], in Southward, London, probate, 1578, PCC

BETHUNE, ALEXANDER, an Ensign of the 46th and later the 49th Regiment, served at Copenhagen and in Holland in 1792-1794. [TNA.WO25.750.218]

ANGLO-DUTCH LINKS, 1560-1860

BEZETH, MARTINUS, from the Netherlands, was naturalised in England on 1 April 1863. [TNA.HO.1.109.4036]

BILLINGTON, JOHN, born 1584, a Separatist from London, with his wife Ellen, born 1588, and sons Francis, born 1606, and John born 1612, a Separatist aboard the Mayflower bound for America in 1620.

BLAGROVE, CHARLES CAMPBELL, son of J. Blagrove of Cardiff Hall, Jamaica, died in Rotterdam on 26 October 1815. [GM.82.671]

BLAGROVE, JONATHAN, was granted a pass to go to Holland and return, on 22 September 1687. [SPDom]

BLYTHE, JAMES, of London, died in Antwerp, [Antwerpen], probate 1582, PCC

BOATSWAINE, JASPER, born 1674 in Le Brill, Holland, settled in Limehouse, London, in 1692, a sailor aboard the Amity from Barbados to London in 1698 and from there to Potuxon, Maryland, in 1699. [TNA.HCA.82]

BOES, MARY, was granted a pass to go to Holland on 24 April 1690. [SPDom.1690.565]

BOEVE, ANDREW, born in Kortricht, Flanders, dwelling in London, probate, 1625, PCC

BOLLE, JAMES, born in Niewkerck, Bollen Bocht, Flanders, dwelling in London, probate, 1622, PCC

BOMINE, ADRIAN, master, and Lucas Daen, pilot, of the Hare of Middelburg bound for San Sebastian, Spain, with munitions, was captured at sea by the Royal Navy in 1590. [SPForeign.169]

BONSY, PHILIP JOSEPH, from Belgium, was naturalised in England on 14 November 1863. [TNA.HO1.112.4247]

BOOGHERT, BARNARD, master of the Prevention trading from Barbados to Surinam in 1679. [TNA]

BOUCXIN, PETER, was granted a pass to go to Niewport or any port in Flanders on 6 December 1687. [SPDom]

BOULDEN, LEWIS, master of the Rachel when bound from Newcastle for London, was captured by the Dutch on 24 July 1663 and imprisoned in Ostend. [Oostende] [SPDom.1663.688]

BOWIN, FRANCIS, master of the Spied Eagle of Bruges arrived in London on 13 December 1567 from Bruges. [Brugge] [TNA.E190.4.2]

BOWSER, ARTHUR, of London, in Southland, Zealand, probate, 1572, PCC

BRADFORD, WILLIAM, born 1589 in Yorkshire, with his wife Dorothy May, born 1597, a Separatist, from Leiden aboard the Speedwell, later aboard the Mayflower bound for America in 1620. Died in Plymouth Colony in 1644.

BRAY, JAMES, a seaman aboard the Rachel when bound from Newcastle for London, was captured by the Dutch on 24 July 1663 and imprisoned in Ostend. [Oostende] [SPDom.1663.688]

BREAME, GEORGE, a citizen and merchant tailor of London, died in Antwerp, [Antwerpen], probate, 1571, PCC

BRETT, JOSEPH, a worsted weaver from Norwich, died in Rotterdam, probate, 1677, PCC

BREWSTER, WILLIAM, born 1566, [died 18 April 1643 in Duxbury, New England], with his wife Mary, born 1568, and children Love, born 1611, and Wrestling, born 1614, a Separatist, from Leiden aboard the Speedwell, later aboard the Mayflower bound for America in 1620. Accompanied by Richard More, born 1613, and Mary More, born 1616.

BRIDGEMAN, AMBROSE, from Westminster, a Major of the 2nd Regiment of Foot Guards, died in Flanders, probate, 1691, PCC

BRITTERIDGE, RICHARD, born 1599, a Separatist in Great Burstead, Essex, from Leiden aboard the Speedwell in 1620, died aboard the Mayflower on 21 December 1620 in Plymouth, New England.

BRONKHURST, JOHN ANTHONY, from the Netherlands, was naturalised in England in 1896. [TNA.HO.144. 386. B20286]

BROUILLE, PETER ANTHONY, was granted a pass to go to Holland on 24 April 1690. [SPDom.1690.565]

BROWN, JAMES, born 1634, was ordained in England in 1660, pastor to a congregation in Ferriby, Yorkshire, in 1677, chaplain to a British congregation in Konigsberg, East Prussia, from 1683 to 1689, moved to Rotterdam in 1689, minister of the Scots Kirk in Rotterdam, from 1691 to 1713, died on 22 November 1713. [F.7.551]

BROWNE, JOHN, born 1582 in Norwich, a courier, licensed to go to the Low Countries in 1637. [TNA]

BROWNE, Sir RICHARD, of Whitehall, London, died in Flanders, probate, 1690, PCC

BROWN, SAMUEL, master of the Violet of Boston from Boston, Lincs., on 4 February 1617 bound for Amsterdam, [TNA.E190. 394.15]

BROWNE, Sir THOMAS, born in London on 19 October 1605, son of Thomas Browne a silk merchant, graduated MD at Leiden. [PC.V.241]

BROWNE, THOMAS, born 1619, from Carlton, Suffolk, licensed to go to Leiden in 1637. [TNA]

BROWN, THOMAS, a mariner purchased the Catt of Amsterdam, in May 1824, in St Sebastians, Spain, from a Flemish skipper imprisoned there, however on his voyage from there he was captured by two Dutch skippers, Andrew Fetherbent and Jacob Adames, who took the ship and its cargo.

BROWNRIGG, WILLIAM, born 24 March 1711, graduated MD from the University of Leiden in 1737, a physician in Whitehaven, Cumberland, died 6 January 1800 in Keswick. [UL]

BRUMONT, FREDERICK, witnessed a deed in New Amsterdam, Berbice, on 14 April 1819. [NRS.RD5.167.185]

BRUNING, FRANCIS, a gentleman from Bambledon, Hampshire, died in Amsterdam, probate, 1699, PCC

BRUNINICK, JOHN, a merchant in London, imported Flemish horses from Rotterdam, a petition, 1664. [SPDom.1664]

BRUNSWICK, MYRTHIL, from Belgium, was naturalised in England on 10 December 1866. [TNA.HO1.136.5280]

BULCKE, PHILLIPE, from Belgium, was naturalised in England on 31 March 1862. [TNA.HO1.104.3770]

BULSTRODE, Sir RICHARD, the English Resident in Brussels, 1685. [SPDom]

BURDETT, Sir WILLIAM VIGORS, when in the Hague, [Den Haag], in 1747, was offered command of a Jacobite regiment to be raised in Support of Prince Charles Edward Stuart. [HO. Pp.1768.1066]

BURKE, W. A., in Surinam, a letter, 1804. [NLS.Adv.ms.47.1.21]

BURR, OLIFF, a merchant in London, trading with Amsterdam in 1567. [TNA.E190.4.2]

BURTON, EDWARD, jr, of London, master of the Sarah and Mary, 270 tons, from Amsterdam to Barbados on behalf of English and Jewish merchants in Amsterdam in 1668. [ActsPCCol.823]

BURTON, WILLIAM, a merchant from Great Yarmouth, settled in Rotterdam in 1661. [Cal.SPDom]

BYAM, WILLIAM, in Surinam, 1660-1670. [BM. South Sea Company. Add.28461]; 'an exact narrative of the state of Guyana and of the English colony in Surynam ......' by William Byam, [Bodleian, ms. Ashmole. 842]; an English planter in Surinam, moved to Antigua in 1668. [Caribbeana.v.2.15]

CAARTEN, PIETER BICKER, from the Netherlands was naturalised in England on 19 November 1860. [TNA.HO.1.98.3401]

CADENNE, HUBERTUS JOSEPHUS BARTHOLEMEUS, from the Netherlands, was naturalised in England on 11 August 1866. [TNA.HO.1.133.5155]

CARON, Sir NOEL, Ambassador of the States General of Belgium, probate, 1628, PCC

CARTWRIGHT, GEORGE, Captain of Villier's Horse, from St Martin-in-the-Fields, London, died in Gelderland on military service, probate, 1699, PCC

CARVER, JACOB, from the Netherlands, was naturalised in England on 10 December 1866. [TNA.HO.1.136.5284]

CATOR, EDWARD, a native of Banbury, established a metal manufacturing works near Rotterdam also near Amsterdam in 1765. [HO.pp.1766.107]

CATS, HARTOG, from the Netherlands, resident of London, was naturalised on 19 April1899. [NRS.HO334.28.10832]

CERF, AMELIA, from Jamaica, daughter of Henry Cerf of Worton Hall, married M. Deby, a barrister from Brussels, in Bath on 9 February 1825. [GM.95.177]

CERF, HENRY, born 1757, late of Isleworth and of Jamaica, died in Brussels on 18 November 1840. [GM.ns.15.110]

CHAMBERLAIN, PETER, MD, one of the King's physicians, was granted a passport to go to Holland on 19 April 1661. [SPDom]

CHAPMAN, ROBERT, born 1600, a weaver in Norwich, was licensed to go to Holland in 1637. [TNA]

CHARLOTT, ARTHUR, was granted a pass to go to Holland and return, on 22 September 1687. [SPDom]

CHECKLIE, JOHN, born 1603, a soldier, licensed to go to Rotterdam on 17 May 1623. [TNA]

ANGLO-DUTCH LINKS, 1560-1860

CHERITON, MARGARET, in Flanders, probate, 1655, PCC

CHRISTIAN, ABRAHAM, a merchant from Middelburg in Zealand, settled in Ireland and was granted denization on 31 December 1667. [BM.ms.Egerton 77]

CLANSONE, CORNELIUS, late of Amsterdam, died overseas aboard the ship Golden Fleece, probate, 1683, PCC

CLARE, PATRICK, a surgeon barber of London, died aboard the Arms of Holland probate1656 PCC

CLARKE, GEDNEY, and his son Gedney, correspondence with William, Count Bentinck the President of the States General of Holland on the affairs of Demerara and Berbice, 1762-1766. [BM.Egerton.1720]

CLARKE, RICHARD, a Separatist, from Leiden aboard the Speedwell, later aboard the Mayflower bound for America in 1620.

CLARKE, SAMUEL, licensed to go to Rotterdam in 1637. [TNA]

CLAIS, CLAUDE, born in Bergen in Hainault, a stranger in London, probate, 1574, PCC

CLAUSZ., PIETER, in the Hook of Enkhuizen, master of the St Pieter, partner with Manuel Rodriques Viega, in a charter party to sail to Dartmouth in England to load a cargo of fish for freight to Porto, Portugal, on 20 August 1598. [TNA.81.45]

CLAYSON, CORNELIS, of the Nightingall of Schiedam, in London, January 1626. [THT.240]

CLAYSON, JOHN, shipper of the White Dove of Medemblik, in London, January 1626. [THT.240]

CLEISON, PETER, master of the Michell of Flushing arrived in London on 10 November 1567 from Flushing; [Vlissingen], master of the Unicorn of Amsterdam arrived in London on 12 December 1567. [TNA.E190.4.2]

CLIFFORD, JEREMY, letters re damage caused by the Dutch Governor and Council of Surinam. [JCTP; 9.1.1704]; an affidavit relating to the estates of Jeremy Clifford in Surinam, 1760. [BM. Newcastle, dd. 32911, f373]; Jeremy Clifford, an English subject, a merchant and planter in Surinam, was prevented in removing his assets from Surinam when it was surrendered by England to the Dutch in 1674, he died in London in 1737, his beneficiaries petitioned the Privy Council, Colonial, on 12 April 1762. [ActsPCCol.477]

COCHETEUX, ANTHONY, a shoemaker from Comen in Flanders, settled in Ireland and granted denization on 9 March 1665. [BM.ms.Egerton 77]

COCKERELL, ROBERT, master of the Peter of Lee arrived in London on 25 November 1567 from Antwerp. [Antwerpen] [TNA.E190.4.2]

COLE, WILLIAM, settled in Rotterdam, was accused of sending arms to England, a petition, 29 February 1663. [SPDom.1664]

COLEPPER, ROGER, son of Anthony Colepepper of Betburye, Kent, formerly Lieutenant of Colepepper's brother, at Delft, probate, 1679, PCC

COMBES, BERTRAND, was imprisoned at The Hague, [Den Haag], then banished from the United Provinces in 1591. [SPForeign.183]

COMBES, JOHN, a shipwright and seaman aboard the Arms of Holland died at sea, probate 1656, PCC

COPCOT, REYNOLD, a citizen and ironmonger of London, died in Zealand, probate, 1608, PCC

COOELLS, JOHN ARENTSO, born in Suijdrecht, Holland, later in South Benfleet, Essex, probate, 1625, PCC

COPPIN, GEORGE, master of the Rejoyce of Boston arrived in Boston, Lincs., in February 1634 from Rotterdam. [TNA.E190.396.1]

COPPIN, JOHN, master of the Robert of Boston, from Boston to Rotterdam on 27 August 1602. [TNA.E190.393.1]

CORNELIS, ADRIAN, master of the Pelican of Amsterdam arrived in London on 8 November 1567. [TNA.E190.4.2]

CORNELIS, ANTHONY, master of the Young Eagle of Antwerp, [Antwerpen], arrived in London on 9 December 1567 from Antwerp, [Antwerpen]. [TNA.E190.4.2]

CORNELIS, CHRISTIAN, master of the Christopher of Antwerp arrived in London on 17 November 1567. [TNA.E190.4.2]

CORNELIS, IBRANDT, master of the Catt of Amsterdam arrived in London on 21 November 1567. [TNA.E190.4.2]

CORNELIS, SEBRANT, master of the George of Purmerend arrived in London on 24 November 1567 from Purmerend. [TNA.E190.4.2]

CORNELIS, TYLMAN, master of the Angel of Amsterdam arrived in London on 31 October 1567 from Amsterdam; master of the Pelican of Amsterdam arrived in London on 15 December 1567 from Amsterdam [TNA.E190.4.2]

CORNELIS, WILLIAM, an apprentice, residing in the parish of St Dunstan in the East, London, in 1694. [CLRO]

CORNELISON, GARRET, was commissioned to recover the dogboat Samaritan of Vlieland which, with its cargo, had been captured by Henry Kirkham who took it to Ireland where it was sold and later brought to Falmouth, England, September 1589. [Cal.SPForeign.iv.99]

CORNELESTON, RICHARD, a Dutch carpenter imprisoned in the Tower of London, bound for the shipyard at Chatham, in November 1670. [SPDom.1670.518]

CORNISH, ANTHONY, master of the Young Eagle of Antwerp [Antwerpen], arrived in London on 27 October 1567. [TNA.E190.4.2]

CORSELIS, MICHEL, born in Roeselaere, Flanders, a merchant in London, probate, 1614, PCC

COSINS, GARRARD, born in Geersburg, Flanders, living in Fenchurch, London, probate, 1627, PCC

COTTON, WILLIAM, a merchant adventurer in Rotterdam, probate, 1655, PCC

ANGLO-DUTCH LINKS, 1560-1860

COX, THOMAS, and his servant, were granted a pass to go to Holland and return on 11 November 1687. [SPDom]

COXE, THOMAS, a turner, with his wife and two children, were permitted to go to and settle in Holland on 14 July 1630. [ActsPC.2.40/157]

CRITOR, PETER, master of the Slake of Flushing, arrived in London on 10 December 1567 from Flushing. [Vlissingen] [TNA.E190.4.2]

CROES, DAVID, a merchant from Gelderland, settled in Ireland and was granted denization on 14 Octobe3r 1664. [BM.ms.Egerton 77]

CROW, HENRY, was authorised to operate a ferry-boat from Maesland Sluys to Harwich in 1661. [SPDom]

CRYNSSEN, ABRAHAM, Commander of the Dutch Fleet, a declaration demanding the surrender of the English colony in Surinam, 20/30 April 1668. [Bodlian, ms.Ashmole, 842.121]

CUBITT, WILLIAM, a worsted weaver from Norwich, died in Holland, probate, 1679, PCC

CUENELLIS, RENIER, of Billeter Lane, St Catherine, Christchurch, London, in Oitzenrode, probate 1575, PCC

CULPEPPER, CHENEY, was granted a pass to go via Harwich to Holland on 22 June 1685. [SPDom]

CURE, WILLIAM, a grant of denization, 10 March 1552. [HSL.7.69]

DACKOMBE, Captain R., in Ostend, a letter, 4 January 1594. [SP.Holland.h132/12]

DA COSTA, ISAAC NUNES, from the Netherlands, was naturalised in England on 29 November 1870. [TNA.HO.1.166.A138]

D'AMOUR, JOHN, a merchant from Amsterdam, was denized in Ireland on 18 April 1670. [BM.ms. Egerton 77]

DANCKERTS, JOHN, a painter in Haarlem, probate, 1686, PCC

DANIEL, WILBERT, a merchant from Flushing [Vlissingen], in Zealand, settled in Ireland and was granted denization on 27 January 1662. [BM.ms. Egerton 77]

DANIELZOON, CORNELIUS, master of the Red Lion of Veere from Boston, Lincs., to Veere on 15 January 1617. [TNA.E190. 394.15]

DARVELL, CORNELIUS, born 1639, a merchant in Amsterdam, [TNA.HCA.78]

DAVIDSON, JAMES, a mariner from Breda in Brabant, settled in Ireland and was granted denization on 13 December 1669. [BM.ms.Egerton 77]

DAVYES, SAMUEL, a merchant of London, imported 46 hundred weight of iron wire from the United Provinces on board a ship of Flushing [Vlissingen], in 1630. [ActsPC.2.40/149]

DE BANCKE, JOSEPH, a citizen and weaver of London, probate 1656 PCC

DE BECKE, LEWIS, a merchant in Amsterdam to be refunded the cargo aboard the Fortune of Hamburg stayed at Dover, England, April 1589. [Cal.SPForeign.iv.99]

DE BRUYNE, LIEVIN, from Ghent [Gent], in Flanders, residing in Lime Street, London, probate, 1573, PCC

DEBY, M., a barrister in Brussels, married Amelia Cerf, daughter of Henry Cerf of Warton Hall, formerly in Jamaica, in Bath, England, on 8 February 1825. [GM.95.177]

DE CARON, Sir NOEL, Ambassador from the States of the United Provinces deceased 1624, his assets were to be administered by Sir Peter Van Lore, Segar Corselles, Lucas Corselles, Abraham Beckes, Mr Burlemachi and Mr Van Der Putt, trustees of the late ambassador, 4 December 1624. [ActsPC.V.393]

DE CLERKE, JOSSE, born in Ghent, [Gent] son of Martin Borne, in East Cheap, London, probate, 1578, PCC

DE CONING, JACOBUS, a merchant in Antwerp, [Antwerpen], trading with Peter Willart, a merchant in London, 1698. [TNA.HCA.82]

DE CONINCKE, JOANNES, minister of the Dutch Church in London, probate, 1627, PCC

DE COSTA, ISAAC NUNES, from the Netherlands, was granted naturalisation in England on 29 November 1870. [TNA.HO.1.166.A138]

DE CRETIS, TROILUS, and his wife Sara, from Antwerp, [Antwerpen], a grant of denization, 10 March 1552. [SPDom]

DE CRITES, JOHN, from Flanders, a grant of denization, 23 March 1604. [HSL.7.56]

DE CRITZ, THOMAS, a gentleman in St Martin in the Fields, probate 1653 PCC

DE CROOKE, ADRIAN, a silk weaver in Whitechapel, probate 1653 PCC

DE CUYPER, SEBASTIAN, son of Henry de Cuyper in Antwerp, [Antwerpen], on Tower Hill, London, probate, 1611, PCC

DE FONSECA, ALONSO, servant of Antonio Fernandes Caravajal a merchant in London, was granted a pass to travel to Flanders on 30 March 1655. [SPDom.1655.580]

DE FREE, WILLIAM, was buried in St Dunstan in the East on 26 October 1743.

DE FRIES, JACOB, was granted denization in England on 21 March 1670. [SPDom.1670]

DE FRISE, GORTIK, master of the Seahen of Amsterdam arrived in London on 6 October 1567 from Danzig. [TNA.E190.4.7]

DE FRY, JOHN, a merchant in Amsterdam, a merchant in Amsterdam to be refunded the cargo aboard the Fortune of Hamburg stayed at Dover, England, April 1589. [Cal.SPForeign.iv.99]

DE GAESBEKE, Baron, from Bruges, [Brugge] married Ellen Claiborne Higham, eldest daughter of Thomas Higham, from Charleston, South Carolina, in Margate, England, on 23 May 1844. [GM.ns.22.86]

ANGLO-DUTCH LINKS, 1560-1860

DE HART, JACQUES, from the Netherlands, was naturalised in England on 29 January 1862. [TNA.HO.1.103.3722]

DE HEERE, MATTHEW, born in Antwerp [Antwerpen], son of Mathew de Heere, a grant of denization 4 June 1581, in London, probate, 1608, PCC. [HSL.7.50]

DE KEYSAR, ANTHONY, a merchant stranger in London, probate, 1573, PCC, London, probate, 1572, PCC

DE KITCH, FRANCIS, master of the Griffin of Dordrecht from Boston, Lincs., on 3 March 1617 bound for Dordrecht. [TNA.E190. 394.15]

DE LA CHAMBRE, DANIEL, Oude Graft, Haarlem, probate, 1690, PCC

DE LA FONTENELLE, ISAAC BENJAMIN, a Lieutenant in Lord Galway's Regiment, died in Flanders, probate, 1694, PCC

DE LE BECQUE, LOUIS, from Kampen, Over Issel, died in Batavia, probate, 1700, PCC

DE LEWE, ADRIAN, master of the Black Lion of Enkhuizen arrived in Boston, Lincolnshire, on 29 August 1602 from Enkhuizen; returned there on 12 September 1602. [TNA.E190.393.1]

DE LA MASEY, JOHN, from Antwerp, [Antwerpen], a mariner aboard the Beaufort, died at sea, probate, 1688, PCC

DE LINDSELL, BARTHOLOMEW, born in Templeure near Tournai, [Kortrijk], and his wife Gomie Cordier, born in Sorle Chasteau in Henaut, both in London, probate, 1610, PCC

DE LIZ, ESTHER, was granted a pass to travel from England to Holland on 6 April 1705. [TNA.SP44.390.417]

DELLON, AGNES, with children, were granted a pass to go to Holland on 25 April 1690. [SPDom.1690.566]

DE LORIE, PETER, a merchant in London, with lands in France and Flanders, probate, 1653, PCC

DE MAY, CATHERINE, widow of Cornelis de Rycke, in Middelburg, probate, 1680, PCC

DE MELLIN, ALEXANDER, born at Houtain near Neville, Brabant, in St Dionis Backchurch, London, probate, 1583, PCC

DE MEULMASTER, JOHN, born in Pytthem, Flanders, later in London, probate, 1607, PCC

DE MEURS, ADRIENNE, widow of Giles Ewens, born in Tournai, later in London, probate, 1610, PCC

DE MILLY, PAUL, a gentleman from the Hague, [Den Haag], was granted denization on18 April 1670. [BM.ms.Egerton 77]

DE MUNCK, BENEDICT, master of the St John trading between the River Thames and Bruges [Brugge] in 1698. [TNA.HCA.82]

DE NICK, FRANCIS, a former burgomaster at Maesland Sluys was authorised to operate a ferry boat from there to Harwich in 1661. [SPDom]

ANGLO-DUTCH LINKS, 1560-1860

DE NIENWERKERK, JACOB CLOOT, in New Amsterdam, Berbice, a deed, 14 April 1819. [NRS.RD5.167.185]

DENNIS, MICHAEL, a merchant from Yperin [Ypres] in Flanders, was granted denization in Ireland on 16 January 1670. [BM.ms. Egerton 77]

DE REUIX, PETER, a merchant from London, in Bruges, [Brugge] probate, 1566, PCC

DERICKSON, CLEYSE, master of the Red Hare of Amsterdam arrived in London on 30 October 1567 from Danzig. [TNA.E190.4.2]

DERICKSON, SIMON, master of the Owl of Haarlem arrived in London on 18 November 1567 from Amsterdam. [TNA.E190.4.2]

DE RIOLES, STEPHEN, in The Hague, [Den Haag], probate, 1700, PCC

DE RUE, BALTHAZAR, a deposition concerning the loading of 191 Africans belonging to the Dutch West India Company, aboard the Golden Sun, master Francis Wier, at Curacao on 27 January 1677. [ActsPCCol.1246]

DE RUITER, MICHAIL, master of the Salamander of Flushing [Vlissingen] bound, with an English convoy, for Barbados and the Caribbee Islands in 1651. [TNA.HCA.30.549]

DE SALMIS, JACOB, a Dutchman, died at the Hague, [Den Haag], probate 1697, PCC

DE SILVA, Sir DUARTE, a gentleman in Antwerp, [Antwerpen], and Lady Blanca de Silva, probate, 1688, PCC

DE SMITH, FRANCIS, a schoolmaster in Flushing, [Vlissingen], died in the parish of St Bartholomew Exchange, London, probate, 1687, PCC

DE STOMBE, JOHANAH, daughter of Phillip and Johanah De Stombe, was baptised in St Dunstan in the East, London, on 26 December 1697.

DE VINCK, JOHN, a merchant in Sandwich, Kent, probate 1655, PCC

DE WASSANAER, Baron, Sieur de Citters, and de Dyckvelt, Ambassadors Extraordinary from the States General, with the Sieur de Wassanaer, the Baron's son, the Sieurs Freeman, Rossem, Pestars, and Ruilemburg, Dr Leaga, and the Sieur Heldever, gentlemen of their retinue, eight pages, three valets de chamber, twelve footmen, a cook, their servants, baggage, utensils, and necessaries to go to Holland, 13 October 1685. [SPDom]

DE WERDE, SYBERTE, a merchant in London, probate, 1559, PCC

DE WEVER, LEWIN, aboard the Blossom, from Barbados to Surinam in December 1679. [TNA]

DE WIKE, BARTOLOMEW, master of the Fortune of Amsterdam arrived in London on 22 December 1567 from Hamburg. [TNA.E190.4.2]

DE WITT, CORNELIUS, was buried in St Michael's, Barbados, on 15 July 1674. [Parish Register]

DES BONURIES, LAURENCE, born in St Gains, Melantois, near Lille, 'in the Low Countries', dwelling in London, probate, 1610, PCC

DES CAMPE, BARBE, widow of John Le Leu, with links to Wombrechie, Flanders, probate, 1655, PCC

DE VISCHER, WILLEM, an investor in the English East India Company, in 1627. [SP.Col.1627.437]

DEWE, RICHARD and JOHN, were permitted to go to Holland and return on 24 July 1685. [SP.Dom]

DIBBETS, FRANCIS, Reformed minister in Dordrecht alias Dort in 1635, returned to England in 1637. [F.7.543]

DIERICH, FRANCIS, born in Antwerp, [Antwerpen], residing in London, probate, 1622, PCC

DIGGS, JOHN, in Rotterdam, possibly from Chilham, Kent, probate, 1656, PCC

DIRICK, ANTHONY, born in Heurn at Tophoven, Masicke, in St Bothulph without Aldgate, London, probate. 1563, PCC

DIRIKSON, GODFREY, master of the Spliedegle of Dordrecht arrived in London on 8 October 1587. [TNA.E190.4.2]

DIRRIKSOON, CLAUS, master of the Red Lion of Amsterdam from Boston, Lincs., on 19 March 1617 bound for Amsterdam. [TNA.E190. 394.15]

DIXI, WOLSTON, a merchant in London trading with Antwerp [Antwerpen], in 1567. [TNA.E190.4.2]

DODD, EDWARD, from the Isle of Man, died at sea off Surinam, probate 1678, PCC

DOHMEN, MARTIN, from the Netherlands, was naturalised in England on 27 January 1871. [TNA.HO.1.171.3]

DORNE, JOHN, master of the Fortune of Antwerp [Antwerpen] arrived in London on 7 October 1567. [TNA.E190.4.7]

DOULDERWAGHER, ADRIAN DRIX, a mariner from Rotterdam, settled in Ireland and was granted denization on 30 April 1669. [BM.ms.Egerton 77]

DOWDALE, GERARD, was granted a pass to go via Dover to Flanders on 27 June 1685. [SPDom]

DRIVER, WILLIAM, a missionary from Shrewsbury, Shropshire, died on St Eustatia in 1813. [GM.83.505]

DROESHOUT, MARTIN, a painter from Brabant, a grant of denization, 30 January 1608. [Cal. SPDom] [HSL.7.63]

DRUEGUER, JONAS, from the Netherlands, was naturalised in England in 1865. [TNA.HO.1.119.4642]

DU CASTEAU, WALRIN, with children in Holland and the Low Countries, probate, 1654, PCC

ANGLO-DUTCH LINKS, 1560-1860

DUCIE, JOHN, in Holland, probate, 1681, PCC

DU CRO, MICHAEL, born in Tournai, [Doornijk]. a merchant in London, probate, 1618, PCC

DUCY, JOHN, late in Holland, probate 1653, PCC

DUDALL, ADRIAN, master of the Falcon of Dordrecht arrived in London on 13 December 1567 from Dordrecht. [TNA.E190.4.2]

DU FOUR, P, in Bergen op Zoom, examination, 31 October 1594. [SP.Holland. xlix. h369/204]

DULAR, BALTHAZAR, was granted a pass to go to Holland on 24 April 1690. [SPDom.1690.565]

DU CARRON, JOSEPH ALEXANDER, from Flanders was naturalised in England on 11 October 1827. [TNA.HO1.9.12]

EARDLIE, THOMAS, possibly from Staffordshire, died in Holland, probate, 1656, PCC

EASTON, Lady DARINGALL, with one gentlewoman, two chambermaids, and two men servants, was granted a pass to go to the Low Countries to join her husband Sir Edward Easton, on 15 June 1624, [ActsPC.V.239]

ELBOROUGH, JEREMIAH, army chaplain at Montfort, minister of the Scots Church in Utrecht from 1627-1629, moved to Hamburg. [F.7.554]

ELLERS, COURT, a merchant in London trading with Amsterdam in 1567. [TNA.E190.4.2]

ELSRAKE, JOSEPH, a Dutchman, a grant of denization, 13 November 1557. [HSL.7.69]

EMKEN, ABRAHAM, from Amsterdam, settled in Ireland and was granted denization on 7 November 1662. [BM.ms.Egerton 77]

EMONDROFF, ..., an apothecary in Maastricht, with links to .... Fullarton in London, 1693. [NRS GD1.885/19]

EMPSELL, WILLIAM, Ensign of Captain Babbington at Bommell in Gelderland, probate, 1680, PCC

ENGLE, PETER, master of the World of Amsterdam arrived in London on 22 November 1567. [TNA.E1904.2]

EVERDOYIS, EVERARD, and his wife Anna Van Den Welde, both burgesses of Antwerp, [Antwerpen], probate, 1565, PCC

EVERTZ, C., Deputy Sheriff in Demerara, witness to a deed, on 20 February 1802. [NRS.RD3.295.657]

EVERWYNS, GERARD, mariner, Jacob Claison, and others of Vleland and Enkhuizen, to be reimbursed for a dogboat with cargo of fish, taken from a Zeeland ship and brought to Sidlesham near Chichester by English pirates, April 1592. [SPForeign.iv.100]

EYKE, CORNELIUS ADRIANSON, in St Buttolphe without Aldgate, London, probate, 1576, PCC

EYRE, JOHN, born 1597, a grocer from Norwich, licensed to go to the Low Countries in 1637. [TNA]

FEBUS, EVERETT, born in Groningen, Friesland, a mariner in Stepney, London, probate, 1656, PCC

ANGLO-DUTCH LINKS, 1560-1860

FENN, JOHN, jr., from Ostend, [Oostende], died in Weymouth, Dorset, probate, 1690, PCC

FENNICK, JOHN, a mariner from The Hague, [Den Haag], Holland, died upon the Loyalty of London in the East Indies, probate, 1691, PCC

FIDLER, JOHN, servant to Henry Sidney, was granted a pass to go to Holland on 10 August 1687. [SPDom]

FIELDING, HENRY, born 22 April 1707 in Sharpham, Somerset, was educated at the University of Leiden in 1728, a novelist, died in Lisbon, Portugal, on 8 October 1754. [UL]

FIEVEZ, THOMAS, from the Netherlands, was naturalised in England on 23 December 1834. [TNA.HO.1.15.29]

FISHER, JOHN, master of the Harry of Lynn, from Boston, Lincs. to Rotterdam on 23 December 1602. [TNA.E190.393.1]

FLEMING, ROBERT, son of Robert Fleming minister of the Scots Church in Leiden, minister of the Scots Church in Rotterdam in 1695, minister of Founder's Hall, London, from 19 June 1698. [F.7.551]

FLETCHER, MOSES, born 1582, a smith from Sandwich, Kent, a Separatist, from Leiden aboard the Speedwell, later aboard the Mayflower bound for America in 1620.

FLORISSON, JACOB, master of the Owl of Dordrecht arrived in London on 3 November 1567 from Dordrecht. [TNA.E190.4.2]

FLOYD, Captain WALTER, at Groningen, a letter, 12 July 1594. [SP.Holland.84.xlix.h285/25]

FORTERIE, ISAAC, chaplain to the army garrison in Utrecht, minister from 1630 until 29 June 1637, returned to England. [F.7.554]

FOSSE, JOHN, of the ship Muden of Amsterdam, probate, 1655, PCC

FOWLSOM, ELIZABETH, born 1610, wife of Thomas Fowlsom in Norwich, licensed to go to Newport in Flanders in 1637. [TNA]

FOXCROFT, ISAAC, a Dutch subject, master of the Carolus Secondus, to bring his ship and family over to England and then to trade with Virginia, 6 February 1674. [ActsPCCol.1038/2]

FRANCES, ADRIAN, master of the Black Falcon of Dordrecht arrived in London on 27 November 1567 from Dordrecht. [TNA.E1904.2]

FRANCIS, PETER, master of the Elizabeth of Dartford arrived in London on 22 December 1567, from Antwerp. [Antwerpen] [TNA.E190.4.2]

FRANSON, ENGLEBERT, of the Hague, [Den Haag], co-owner of the Rich Dollar of Rotterdam with its cargo of salt and fish, captured by [English?] pirates, a commission, August 1590. [SPForeign.iv.99]

FRANSON, JACQUES, born in Antwerp, [Antwerpen], son of Govert Franson, in London, probate, 1605, PCC

FREDERICI, ..., Governor of Surinam, a letter, 1801. [NRS.GD46.17.20]

FREEHILL, WILLIAM, a surgeon from Dort, [Dordrecht], Holland, died aboard the ship Fellowship, probate, 1695, PCC

FREXEN, AUGUSTINE, minister of the Anglican Church in Dordrecht, was granted a pass to go to Holland on 18 June 1685. [SPDom]

FRYSE, MARTEN, master of the Samson of Bruges arrived in London on 1 October 1567 from Bruges [Brugge]. [TNA.E190.4.7]

GALEARDO, PAWLE, a servant of the Queen in Antwerp, [Antwerpen], probate, 1563, PCC

GALMBERT, GUSTAVE ALFRED HIPPOLYTE, from Belgium, was naturalised in England on 21 December 1854. [TNA.HO1.59.1936]

GARARD, JEREMY, a merchant, was granted a pass to go to Holland and return, on 17 April 1672. [SPDom.1672.335]

GABRY, JOHN, born in Tournai, [Kortrijk], son of James Gabry, a merchant, residing in London, probate, 1605, PCC

GARDNER, JOHN, a gentleman from London, died in Flanders, probate, 1692, PCC

GARETSON, JACOB, master of the Jerusalem of Amsterdam arrived in London on 3 October 1567 from Amsterdam. [TNA.E190.4.7]

GARETSON, JOHN, master of the Nightingale of Amsterdam arrived in London on 3 October 1567 from Amsterdam. [TNA.E190.4.7]

GARETSON, LUCAS, master of the Black Dragon of Amsterdam arrived in London on 17 November 1567 from Amsterdam; master of the Half Moon of Amsterdam arrived in London on 15 December 1567 from Amsterdam. [TNA.E190.4.2]

GARNETT, MARY, widow of Henry Garnett late of The Brill, Holland, now resident of King's Lynn, Norfolk, probate, 1625, PCC

GASPOOLE, JOHN, a gentleman from Louvain, Brabant, in Westham, Essex, probate, 1624, PCC

GASCOYNE, Sir BERNARD, via Harwich to Holland on 26 February 1672. [SPDom.1672.167]

GEARE, ROBERT, in Amsterdam, probate, 1679, PCC

GEGONDEE, JOHN, in Brussels, probate, 1679, PCC

GERNAT, FRANCOIS, from Belgium, was naturalised in England on 12 March 1857. [TNA.HO1.79.2399]

GERRARD, MARTIN, from Holland, a goldsmith in London, a grant of denization, 18 November 1535. [HSL.7.55]

GERRITSON, CORNELIUS, born in Rotterdam, a mariner, naturalised in England on 7 January 1668. [Cal.SPDom]

GERETSON, GERRETT, born in Wicke Duersteend by Utrecht, residing in Duke's Place, London, probate, 1625, PCC

GILL, ISAAC, a merchant from Flushing, [Vlissingen], Holland, settled in Ireland and was granted denization on 18 July 1666. [BM.ms.Egerton 77]

GILLSTOUT, JOHN, from Amsterdam, died at sea aboard the Robert and William, probate, 1696, PCC

GILMAN, ANTHONY, born 1734, a merchant in London, with Leonora Gilman, born 1744, and three children, via London aboard the Benjamin and Mary, bound for Veere, Zealand, in August 1774. [TNA.T47.9/11]

GIRDLESTONE, THOMAS, born 1758 in Holt, Norfolk, a student at the University of Leiden in 1787, a physician in Great Yarmouth, died 25 June 1822. [UL]

GLAZIER, THOMAS, a gentleman from London, died aboard the Arms of Holland, probate 1656 PCC

ANGLO-DUTCH LINKS, 1560-1860

GOODHAND, LEONARD, a gentleman from Algerkirke, Holland, in Lincolnshire, probate, 1689, PCC

GOODMAN, JOHN, born 1595, a linen weaver, a Separatist, from Leiden aboard the Speedwell, later aboard the Mayflower bound for America in 1620.

GORDON, WILLIAM, Minister Plenipotentiary at Brussels in 1766. [HO pp.1766.148]

GOSSCHALK, EDWARD, from the Netherlands, was naturalised in England on 13 June 1866. [TNA.HO.1.131.5072]

GOOSSEN, LEONARD, from Utrecht, later in London, probate, 1605, PCC

GOULD, THOMAS, a mariner on HMS Adventure at Helversluis, probate, 1693, PCC

GRACE, GEORGE, a merchant in London and Delft, trading with Virginia in 1635. [TNA.E190.8.1][SPDom16.475]

GREENE, EDMUND, master of Mary Adventure burnt by the Dutch on the River Elbe in 1666, a petition by Elizabeth Birstall his widow in 1672. [SPDom.1672.237]

GREES, MARY, was granted a pass to go to Holland on 24 April 1690. [SPDom.1690.565],

GREGORIE, JOHN, in Veere, referred to in the Will of Robert Elliot in Demerara, a merchant in Christiansted, St Croix, witnessed a deed there on 13 April 1821. [NRS.RD5.204.550]

GRIGGS, JOHN, born 1788, son of James Griggs in Enfield, Middlesex, a surgeon, died in Surinam on 25 December 1809. [GM.79.478]

GRISPER, CHARLES HENRIQUE, was granted a pass to go to Flanders on 25 April 1690. [SPDom.1690.566]

GROAT, WILLIAM JOHNSON, a mariner in Medlee, Holland, probate, 1679, PCC

GROOS, CARL WILHELM, from the Netherlands, residing in London, was naturalised in 1889. [TNA.HO334.16.6033]

GUION, JOANES, born 1774 in Curacao, died 1 June 1827. [Spring Path, Kingston, Jamaica, gravestone]

GULICKER, PETERNEL, was granted a pass to go to Holland on 24 April 1690. [SPDom.1690.565]

GUNTER, JOHN, a Presbyterian minister from Woodstock, Oxford, an assistant at the Scots Church in Rotterdam from 1723, ordained there on 20 October 1730, died 18 April 1736, buried in the Prince's Kirk in Rotterdam. [F.7.551]

GURDSON, or JOHNSON, JACOB, of Calfer Deecke in Holland, died aboard the Lyon in Plymouth Sound, 'in State service', probate, 1656, PCC

HAAS, JULIUS JOHANN ROBERT, from the Netherlands was naturalised in England on 6 September 1862. [TNA.HO.1.106.3909]

HALL, BENEDICT, of Highmeadow, Gloucestershire, died at Cambrai, Flanders, his widow Anne Hall, probate 1684, PCC

HALL, JOHN, master of the Falcon of Newcastle, a pirate, captured the Abye of Amsterdam, master Thomas Upton, on 15 September 1575.

HAMILTON, GEORGE, from Westminster, later in Flanders, probate, 1692, PCC

HANSON, HANS, master of the Fortune of Flushing, [Vlissingen], arrived in Boston, Lincolnshire, on 2 December 1602 from Bordeaux. [TNA.E190.393.1]

HARBIN, CHARLES, from Yeovil, Somerset, died in Maastricht, probate, 1691, PCC

HARDENBERG, FRANCIS JOHN, from the Netherlands, was naturalised in England on 27 October 1865. [TNA.HO.1.125.4858]

HARLOE, JOHN, a Dutch subject, master of the Charitas to bring his ship and family over to England and then to trade with Virginia, 6 February 1674. [ActsPCCol.1038/2]

HARRIS, JOHN, a merchant in London, shipped goods aboard the White Angel, master Jacob Lauwer van Slot, from Virginia bound for Amsterdam in June 1659, however the ship was captured by a privateer based in St Sebastian, Spain. [CLRO.Depositions]

HARRIS, JOHN, a merchant, having lost his own ship by fire at Bridgetown, Barbados, petitioned to hire the Endracht, master John Johnson, to sail to Barbados and return with timber to the Port of London, 26 June 1668. [ActsPCCol.780]

HARRIS, WILLIAM, master of the Edward of Milton arrived in London on 6 December 1567 from Antwerp. [Antwerpen] [TNA.E190.4.2]

HARRISON, ... of Beverley, an English pirate, captured the Andrew of Amsterdam, master David Weyd, on 4 July 1574. [SPDom]

HARTLEY, ROGER, a merchant in Rotterdam, probate, 1653, PCC

HARTLEY, WILLIAM, and his wife Elizabeth Van Der Lane, both of Rotterdam, probate, 1697, PCC

HARVEY, Sir JAMES, an Alderman of London, with links to Antwerp, [Antwerpen], probate, 1583, PCC

HARWELL, NICHOLAS, 'horseman of the Rittmaster Sir Ratcliffe' in the garrison at Niemeghen, [Nijmegen] probate, 1610, PCC

HATTON, CHRISTOPHER, born 1601 in Bradish in Norfolk, a pot seller of earthen vessels, licensed to go to Holland in 1637. [TNA]

HATTON, ROBERT, from Barbados aboard the sloop Hunter, master Walter Assueron, bound for Surinam on 3 March 1679. [TNA]

HAY, JEANNA, eldest daughter of Adolphus Hay, married John Christian Bowring from Guadaloupe-y-Calvo, Mexico, in Antwerp [Antwerpen], on 11 November 1843. [GM.ns.23.91]

HAYWARD, JACOB SCOTT, a coffee planter in Dutch Guiana, diary, 1840-1842. [per Hayward's End, Gloucester]

HAYWARD, JOSEPH, born 1608, a dorinx weaver in Norwich, with his wife Susanna, born 1611, and servant Esther Brown, born 1616, licensed to go to Rotterdam in 1637. [TNA]

HEATH, EDWARD, master of the Magdalen of Newhaven, was shipping ordnance from Lewes, England, to Flushing [Vlissingen], illegally in 1591. [SPForeign.180]

HEDRICKES, PETER, master of the Jonas of Middelburg to sequester the cargo of the Mogador of Barbary taken by George Ryman, captain of the Scout and taken to Portsmouth, England, May 1589. [Cal.SP.Foreign, iv.99]

HEESTER, JAMES, a merchant from Holland, settled in Ireland and was granted denization on 27 January 1662. [BM.ms.Egerton 77]

HERBECQ, FELIX, from Belgium, was naturalised in England on 24 November 1853. [TNA.HO1.52.1683]

HERBERT, MAGNUS MORTON, from Nevis, died in Brussels on 31 October 1834. [GM.105.446]

HERLOGS, JOSEPH, from Belgium, was naturalised in England on 12 July 1864. [TNA.HO1.116.4447]

HERRING, JULIUS, a Puritan minister at St Alkmund's, Shrewsbury, Shropshire, minister of the Reformed Church in Amsterdam from 1637 until his death in 1645. [F.7.538]

HERWYN, JACOB, an investor in the English East India Company in 1627. [SP.Col.1627.437]

HICKMAN, HENRY, minister of the Gospel in English, in Leiden, probate, 1693, PCC

HICKMAN, alias STRODE, JOANNA, a widow in Leiden, probate, 1693, PCC

HIGHAM, ELLEN CLAIBORNE, eldest daughter of Thomas Higham in Charleston, South Carolina, married Baron de Gaesbeke, from Bruges, [Brugge] Flanders, in Margate, Kent, on 23 May 1844. [GM.ns.22.86]

HILL, JOHN, an articifer in iron and steel manufacture, especially coach springs, established a workshop in Rhoon-in-the-Overmaasel, near Rotterdam, also employed at Edward Cator's works at Op de Overtoonse Weg, a mile and a half from Amsterdam in 1765. [TNA.HO.pp.107]

HILL, THOMAS, a gentleman from Aldgate, London, died in The Hague, Den Haag], probate, 1629, PCC

HODGE, ALEXANDER, a Fellow of Wadham College, Oxford, minister of St Thomas's in Exeter, ejected as a Puritan, fled to Holland, minister of the English Reformed Church in Delft in 1668, then in Amsterdam from 1669 to 1689, probate, 1690, PCC, [F.7.538/543]

ANGLO-DUTCH LINKS, 1560-1860

HODGE, MARGARET, a widow from Baestunerye, [Holland?], later in Essex, probate, 1581, PCC

HODGES, JAMES, from London, died in Rotterdam, probate, 1689, PCC

HOFFEMEISTER, JOHN DANIEL, was granted a pass to go to Holland on 6 June 1685. [SPDom]

HOLDICHE, EDMOND, intent to travel to the Low Countries, probate, 1606, PCC

HOLMAN, HARMAN, from Antwerp, [Antwerpen], in St Catherine Colman, London, probate, 1582, PCC

HODSKIN, ALEXANDER, a merchant in Amsterdam, probate, 1653, PCC

HOLDTSHOE, HERMAN, a merchant stranger in London, probate, 1616, PCC

HOLLES, MACCABEUS, was despatched to Holland to gain intelligence regarding the Dutch fleet, on 23 April 1672. [SP.Dom.1672.610]

HOOKE, JOHN, born 1606, a servant to Isaac Allerton, a Separatist, from Leiden aboard the Speedwell, later aboard the Mayflower bound for America in 1620, died 1621.

HORONSEN, GARRETT, a bachelor who died in Barbados, Admin.1657, PCC

HORST, JOHANN ADAM, from the Netherlands, was naturalised in England on 14 March 1862. [TNA.HO.1.103.3747]

HOWARD, Dame WALBURGA WANDEN, in The Hague, [Den Haag], probate, 1690, PCC

HUBEAU, PIERRE JOSEPH, from Belgium, was naturalised in England on 9 June 1867. [TNA.HO1.141.5509]

HUDSON, ANTHONY, master of the Robert of Lyn from Boston, Lincolnshire, to Amsterdam on 24 October 1601. [TNA.E190.393.1]

HUGHES, Colonel, of the 87th Regiment, in Curacao, a letter 1801. [NRS.GD46.17.20]

HUITT, LEONARD, a clothworker of London, in Antwerp, [Antwerpen], probate, 1565, PCC

HUSSCHER, GILES, from Bruges, [Brugge] Flanders, later in London, probate, 1560, PCC

HUTCH, JOSEPH, master of the .... of Sandwich, when bound from Vlissingen, [Flushing], was captured by privateers from Dunkirk in 1624; similarly, he, on the Sea Horse of Sandwich, was captured by privateers of Vlissingen and taken to Niewpoort in Flanders on 20 April 1624. [ActsPC.V.239]

HYDE, SARAH, widow of Samuel Lodge, in Surinam, probate, 1699, PCC

ISAACS, LEWIS, from the Netherlands, was naturalised in England on 24 July 1854. [TNA.HO.1.56.1847]

ISBRANT, GARET, master of the Green Cloverblade of Amsterdam arrived in London on 17 November 1567. [TNA.E190.4.2]

ISRAEL, ANTHONY, master of the Fortune of Amsterdam, arrived in Boston on 22 October 1611 from Amsterdam; from Boston, Lincs., bound for St Malo on 2 May 1617. [TNA.E190. 394.15]

JACOB, HENRY, born 1563 in Chariton, Kent, educated at Oxford University in 1580s, moved to Holland in 1593, a pastor in Middelburg, Zeeland, a Congregationalist minister in London from 1616 to 1620, emigrated to Virginia in 1622, died in London in 1624.

JACOBS, JOOS, a mariner from Zierikzee, then in Stepney, London, aboard the Anne, probate, 1690, PCC

JACOBSON, ADRIAN, master of the Black Raven of Purmerend arrived in London on 12 November 1567. [TNA.E190.4.2]

JACOBSON, FLORIS, master of the Spledegle of Amsterdam arrived in London on 25 November 1567 from Amsterdam. [TNA.E1904.2]

JACOBSON, JACOB, master of the Hoy Wagon of Amsterdam arrived in London on 11 December 1567. [TNA.E190.4.2]

JAMESON, EDWARD, Commissary of the States General at Cork, a letter, 1795. [NRS.GD51.2.37.1-2]

JANSE, MARTYNTIE, was granted a pass to go to Holland on 24 April 1690. [SPDom.1690.565]

JANSEN, CLAYSE, cook of the Nightingale of Schiedam in London, January 1626. [THT.240]

JANSEN, NICHOLAS, a mariner from Holland, aboard the ship Elizabeth and Mary, probate 1695, PCC

JANSEN, PAUL, a merchant from Antwerp, [Antwerpen], dwelling in Amsterdam, probate, 1608, PCC

JANSEN, PETER, from the Netherlands, was naturalised in England on 2 September 1863. [TNA.HO.1.111.4170]

JEROENSON, JEROEN, a Dutch subject, master of the Liefde to bring his ship and family over to England and then to trade with Virginia, 6 February 1674. [ActsPCCol.1038/2]

JOB, CORNELIUS, son of Cornelius and Micheley Job, was baptised in St Katherine by the Tower, London, on 22 January 1693.

JODRELL, JOHN, a Captain in Princess Anne of Denmark's Regiment of Foot, in Dixmuyde, Flanders, probate, 1693, PCC

JOHNSON, ABEL, son of John Johnson in Groningen, Friesland, died at sea on board the Love of London, Captain Elias Jordon, bound for the East Indies, probate, 1656, PCC

JOHNSON, ADRIAN, of the Hague, [Den Haag], co-owner of the Rich Dollar of Rotterdam with its cargo of salt and fish, captured by [English?] pirates, a commission, August 1590. [SPForeign.iv.99]

JOHNSON, BOWEN, boatswain of the Nightingale of Schiedam in London, January 1626. [THT.240]

JOHNSON, CHARLES, from London, died in Flanders, Probate, 1692, PCC

JOHNSON, CLEISE, master of the Christopher of Dordrecht arrived in London on 17 November 1567. [TNA.E190.4.2]

JOHNSON, DAVIE, master of the Buckett of Flushing arrived in London on 8 December 1567 from Flushing. [Vlissingen] [TNA.E190.4.2]

JOHNSON, FRANCIS, master of the Falcon of Flushing arrived in London on 30 October 1567 from Flushing. [Vlissingen] [TNA.E190.4.2]

JOHNSON, HENRIK, master of the Mychell of Amsterdam arrived in London on 8 October 1567 and on 15 December 1567 from Amsterdam. [TNA.E190.4.2]

JOHNSON, JORGEN, possibly from Herrne, Holland, died at sea on board the Anne Bon Adventure, master Christopher Paige, probate, 1655, PCC

JOHNSON, LAWRENCE, from Horne, Holland, a mariner aboard the Daniel and Thomas of London bound for Madagascar, probate 1688, PCC

JOHNSON, LEONARD, master of the Pelican of Antwerp, [Antwerpen], arrived in London on 22 December 1567 from Antwerp, [Antwerpen]. [TNA.E190.4.2]

JOHNSON, MARGARET, a widow, Cornelius van Campen, and …. Frouse of Rotterdam to receive their fisher boat and its furniture which had been taken at sea and brought to Dartmouth, England, October 1589. [Cal.SPForeign.iv.99]

JOHNSON, MARTEN, master of the Popingaye of Haarlem arrived in London on 17 October 1567. [TNA.E190.4.2]

JOHNSON, NANINCK, master of the Unicorn of Haarlem arrived in London on 17 October 1567 from Arnemuiden. [TNA.E190.4.2]

JOHNSON, PETER, master of the Jacob of Arnemuiden arrived in London on 11 November 1567. [TNA.E190.4.2]

JOHNSON, PETER, master of the Black Eagle of Antwerp [Antwerpen], arrived in London on 14 November 1567. [TNA.E190.4.2]

JOHNSON, VINCENT, master of the Falcon of Antwerp [Antwerpen] arrived in London on 22 November 1567. [TNA.E1904.2]

JOHNSON, VISSELL, of All Hallows, Barking, London, in Zealand, probate, 1581, PCC

JONES, ROGER, an English subject, formerly in Surinam, a prisoner aboard a Dutch man'o'war at the Isle of Wight, 2 December 1668. [ActsPCCol.814]

JOYCE, SIMON, master of the James of Antwerp [Anteerpen] arrived in London on 3 December 1567 from Antwerp. [Antwerpen] [TNA.E190.4.2]

JOYSON, ANTHONY, master of the Bonaventure of Antwerp [Antwerpen], arrived in London on 3 October 1567 from Antwerp; also, on 24 November 1567. [TNA.E190.4.7]

JUDA, SOLOMON, a Jew, who killed a soldier near Rotterdam, to be returned to Holland for trial, 1769. [TNA.HO. pp.1766.1177]

JUNIUS, FRANCIS, from The Hague, [Den Haag], died in Datchet, Buckinghamshire, probate, 1678, PCC

JURIANSON, JOHN, master of the Catt of Haarlem arrived in London on 10 October 1567 from Haarlem. [TNA.E190.4.2]

JURIANS, PETER, a mariner from Cawdon in Friesland, was granted denization in Ireland on 15 June 1671. [BM.ms.Egerton 77]

KELSEY, THOMAS, was permitted to go to Holland and bring his family and goods back from there, 23 January 1672. [SPDom.1672.98]

KARMANS, BALTHASAR, from Antwerp, [Antwerpen], a grant of denization, 8 June 1566. [HSL.7.71]

KENNERS, LIVIN ANTHONY EMMANUEL, from Belgium, was naturalised in England on 29 February 1864. [TNA.HO1.113.4301]

KENRICK, EDWARD, a merchant adventurer of England, in Rotterdam, probate, 1654, PCC

KEY, RICHARD, a merchant, was granted a pass to go to Holland on 9 October 1687. [SPDom]

KILLIGREW, JAMES, in Ghent, [Gent], probate, 1693, PCC

KIPS, JOSEPH, from Belgium, was naturalised in England on 8 January 1866. [TNA.HO1.128.4930]

KNAPPE, EDMUND, born 1612 in Great Killingham, a gentleman there, licensed to go to Holland 'to serve the States', on 28 March 1637. [TNA]

KNIGHT, THOMAS, aboard the Arms of Holland sent home on the Wildman from the West Indies as disabled, probate 1656, PCC

KOEKKOCH, HERMANUS, from the Netherlands, was naturalised in England on 14 July 1866. [TNA.HO.1.132.5123]

KUYPERS, CAREL NICOLAS PETER, from the Netherlands, was naturalised in England on 7 November 1863. [TNA.HO.1.112.4217]

KYNTE, ELIZABETH, with her son, two daughters, and a maid servant, were permitted to go to Delft on 1 June 1630. [PC.2.40/54]

LADD, CATHERINE, a spinster from Leiden, Holland, died in Stoke Newington, probate, 1695, PCC

LAET, MELCHIOR, from London, in Antwerp, [Antwerpen], probate, 1570, PCC

LAMBARD, WILLIAM, was licensed to go to Holland in 1637. [TNA]

LAMBERT, CHRISTOPHE R, jr., born in Perne, Tournoi, [Kortrijk], son of Christopher Lambert, later in Coleman Street, London, probate, 1609, PCC

LAMBERT, CHRISTOPHER, born in Sachin, Tournoi, [Kortrijk], son of Ciro Lambert, later in Coleman Street, London, probate, 1609, PCC

LAMBRIT, alias GENNYNG, THOMAS, born in the Bishopric of Liege, [Luik], residing in Ludgate, London, probate, 1562, PCC

LANGFORD, THOMAS, died in The Hague, [Den Haag], probate, 1684, PCC

LANGLEY, THOMAS, in Holland to gain intelligence concerning the Dutch fleet at Helvoetsluis, Rotterdam, Brill, Amsterdam, the Texel, and Zealand, a letter from the Hague, [Den Haag], 14 March 1672. [SPDom.Car.ii.303/235a]

LAWRENCE, JACOB, master of the Jacob of Antwerp, [Antwerpen], arrived in London on 22 November 1567. [TNA.E1904.2]

LEDEBOER, HERMAN ARNOLD, from the Netherlands, residing in Fallowfield, was naturalised in 1879. [TNA.HO334.9.3004]

LEE, JOHN, a gentleman from London, died in Flanders, probate, 1692, PCC

ANGLO-DUTCH LINKS, 1560-1860

LE FEBURE, JOHN, born in Tournai, [Kortrijk], a merchant in London, probate, 1610, PCC

LE BRUN, JAMES, was granted a pass to go to Holland on 24 April 1690. [SPDom.1690.565]

LE KEUX, JONAS, in Canterbury, possibly from Flushing [Vlissingen] in Holland, probate, 1656, PCC

LEMAN, MICHAEL, as procurator of Lawrence Backe, Francis Granier, John Granier, and other merchants of Holland and Zeeland, was commissioned to recover 'sundry Flanders commodities of great value' taken by Captain John Stratford and taken to Plymouth, England, in November 1590. [SPForeign.iv.99]

LEMAN, MICHAEL, and Harman Rodenbroughe were commissioned to return the cargo of the Romier taken in May1590 by John Clerk, captain of the Roebuck and taken to Plymouth, England, January 1592. [SPForeign.iv.100]

LEMAN, MICHAEL, on behalf of John Granier, Francis Granier, Cornelius Minnis, Balthasar Moucheron, and others, was commissioned to restore the cargo of the Rider and of the Dolphin master Abraham Garretson, taken by John Stratford, captain of the Minton of Bristol and by John Markham captain of the Segar of London, February 1592. [SPForeign.iv.100]

LEMAN, MICHAEL, was granted a commission to restore to Cornelius Cornelison the Jonas of Amsterdam and its cargo which was taken by William Batten, captain of the Prudence of Barnstaple and brought to Barnstaple, England, May 1592. [SPForeign.iv.100]

LEMAN, MICHAEL, Agent for the States of Holland and Zeeland, was commissioned to compensate for a ship of Amsterdam and its cargo from Spain captured by Humphrey Fryer captain of the <u>Pleasure of Bristol</u> an taken to Penzance in England, March 1593. [SPForeign.iv.100]

LEMAN, MICHAEL, Agent for the States of Holland and Zealand, was commissioned to restore the cargo of the <u>Growing Moon</u> taken by Henry Thyn and John Glenville, March 1593. [SPForeign.iv.100]

LEMAN, MICHAEL, on behalf of Isaac le Maier and other merchants of Amsterdam also John Johnson master and ownerof the <u>Sampson of Olre in Holland</u> for goods lost through shipwreck, July 1593. [SPForeign.iv.100]

LEMAN, MICHAEL was commissioned, on behalf of Jasper Tradell, Pete Bullard, Michael le Fort, and other merchants of Middelburg, to compensate for their loss when the <u>Salamander of Flushing</u> [Vlissingen], was shipwrecked on the coast of Cumberland and the cargo taken by Richard Luther, Thomas Charlton and others, February 1594. [SPForeign.iv.100]

LEMAN, MICHAEL and LIVEN DE HAISTE, on behalf of Robert de la Barr, David le Maire, Peter de Coster, and Francis le Fort, merchants of London, James de Hawse and Claes Johnson Brune and others, merchants of Holland and Zealand for cargo aboard the <u>Golden Lion of Middelburg</u> and the <u>Red Lion of London</u> cast away on the Goodwin Sands, July 1594. [SPForeign.iv.101]

LENSSEIR, or LENSSEN, JACOB, in Gravesend, Kent, probate, 1571, PCC, linked to the Dutch church in London.

ANGLO-DUTCH LINKS, 1560-1860

LEVISTON, Dame MARGARET, with her son, two daughters and servants were permitted to go to The Hague, [Den Haag], on 11 June 1630. [ActsPC.2.40/55]

LEVY, MOISE, from the Netherlands, was naturalised on 4 May 1871. [TNA.HO334.1.337]

LEVY, MOSES GOULOUPER, from the Netherlands, was naturalised in England on 11 July 1865. [TNA.HO.1.122.4756]

LINCKEBEECK, HANS CORNELIUS, a merchant in London, from Amsterdam or Leiden, probate, 1655, PCC

LIND, MATTHYS, born a Dutchman, was permitted 'to go beyond the seas' on 24 July 1685. [SPDom]

LINSON, CORNELIUS, master of the Ruby of Flushing [Vlissingen], to have his ship returned which had been taken and brought to Saltash, England, by Robert Flick, captain of the Merchant Royal, June 1589. [Cal.SPForeign.iv.99]

LLOYD, Colonel EDWARD, from Westminster, died in s'Hertogenbosch, Brabant, when on His Majesty's Service, 1695, PCC

LOEMAN, MARY and HESSEBA, were granted passes to go to Holland on 21 July 1685. [SPDom]

LONGUEVILLE, DAVID, graduated MA from Edinburgh University in 1730, a minister in Exeter, minister of the Scots Church in Amsterdam from 1740 until his death in 1776. [F.7.538]

LOWE, STEPHEN, a mariner from London, aboard HMS Garland in Holland, probate, 1693, PCC

LUCAS, FRANCIS and ANDREW, merchants aboard the Hawk of Muscovy of Amsterdam at Carrickfergus on September 1615. [Temple Newsam mss, West Yorkshire Archives]

LUPTON, THOMAS, master of the William of Wainfleet, from Boston, Lincs. to Middelburg on 27 August 1602. [TNA.E190.393.1]

LUTTON, H. C., witnessed a deed in New Amsterdam, Berbice, on 14 April 1819. [NRS.RD5.167.185]

LYMPET, PAUL, master of the Romaine of Antwerp, [Antwerpen], arrived in London on 8 December 1567. [TNA.E190.4.2]

LYNDT, JAN, a mariner from Amsterdam, died aboard the merchant ship King William in the precincts of St Katherine-by-the-Tower, London, probate, 1698, PCC

LYNES, ANDREW, master of the Jolly Owl of Harlingen arrived in London on 24 November 1567 from Harlingen. [TNA.E1904.2]

MACKENZIE, THOMAS, from Barbados, died 1831 in Dunkirk. [GM.101.652]

MADEN, RICHARD, minister at Utrecht from 1645 to 1647, Emeritus in 1666, died in June 1680. [F.7.538]

ANGLO-DUTCH LINKS, 1560-1860

MAELSTAFF, PETER, in Ostend, [Oostende] Flanders, probate, 1681, PCC

MAGENIS, ARTHUR, and 20 other soldiers, formerly of the King's Guards, granted permission to go to Flanders, 23 January 1668. [Cal.SPDom]

MAGHIR, MARGARET, and her son, were permitted to go to her husband in The Hague, [Den Haag], 3 April 1631. [PC.2.40/812]

MAHIEU, ARNOLD, from Belgium, was naturalised in England on 20 August 1845. [TNA.HO1.19.204]

MAILLETT, alias ANTHONIE, MARIANA, a widow from Rotterdam, died overseas, probate, 1696, PCC

MALLEBRAMEG, JAMES, a merchant in Haarlem Straat, Leyden, Holland, probate, 1681, PCC

MANSHART, MARIA, a Dutch woman, was granted a pass to go to Holland on 25 April 1690. [SPDom.1690.566]

MANTEAN, LEWIS, born in Bergen-op-Zoom, in London, probate, 1570, PCC

MARGERSON, EDWARD, a Separatist, from Leiden aboard the Speedwell, later aboard the Mayflower bound for America in 1620.

MARIEN, FRANCIS, from Belgium, was naturalised in England on 22 March 1859. [TNA.HO1.89.2879]

MARION, JACOB, a merchant in Amsterdam, probate, 1685, PCC

ANGLO-DUTCH LINKS, 1560-1860

MARSHALL, JOHN, from London, died in The Hague, [Den Haag], probate,1695, PCC

MARSHALL, Dr THOMAS, arrived at Scheveling on 18 December 1671, wrote from Dordrecht on 26 December, to negotiate with Mr Van Dyke of Amsterdam, a letter. [SPDom.1672.72]

MARSON, JOHN, master of the Browne of Haarlem arrived in London on 4 December 1567 from Haarlem. [TNA.E190.4.2]

MASMAN, MICHAEL, master of the Nightingale of Veere arrived in Boston, Lincolnshire on 3 May 1602. [TNA.E190.393.1]

MASSHYESEZ, JANNETIE, was granted a pass to go to Holland on 24 April 1690. [SPDom.1690.565]

MATHEENSON, JAMES, from Breda, in St Pulchers without Newgate, London, probate, 1570, PCC

MATON, ADELE, from Belgium, was naturalised in England on 23 November 1868. [TNA.HO1.153.6009]

MATTHYSSENS, EDWARD, from Belgium, was naturalised in England on 6 March 1846. [TNA.HO1.21.335]

MAURITZ, JACOB, born 1645 in Harlem, Holland, a mariner who settled in New York in 1659. [TNA.HCA.80]

MAUROIS, ELIAS, born in Houpelinnes in the Low Countries, now in Canterbury, probate, 1629, PCC

MAYNOUR, KATHERINE, born in Antwerp, [Antwerpen], Brabant, a widow and a painter, was granted denization in England on 9 November 1540. [HSL.7]

ANGLO-DUTCH LINKS, 1560-1860

MEAD, RICHARD, born 11 August 1673 in London, a physician, educated at the Universities of Utrecht and Leiden, died in London on 16 February 1754. [UL]

MEOLES, HENRY, sr., Captain of a Company of Foot soldier in the Netherlands, dwelling in The Hague, [Den Haag], probate PCC, 1654,

MEOLES, JOHN, in The Hague, [Den Haag], probate, 1654, PCC

MERRICKE, RICHARD, from Naumegan [Nijmegen], in Gelderland, settled in Ireland and was granted denization on 27 January 1662. [BM.ms.Egerton 77]

MERCHAND, GERARD, was granted a pass to go to Holland on 25 April 1690. [SPDom.1690.566]

MESSE, PETER, master of the Mearman of Amsterdam arrived in London on 4 December 1567 from Amsterdam. [TNA.E190.4.2]

MONGEY, MONACHA, a widow in St Mary Wolmar, London, from Antwerp, [Antwerpen], probate, 1570, PCC

MORTIMER, Mr, British Vice Consul in Ostend, [Oostende], in 1766. [HO pp.148.148]

MYCHELLS, CORNILIS, master of the James of Flushing, [Vlissengen], arrived in London on 24 December 1567. [TNA.E190.4.2]

MICHELLSON, MARTIN, master of the Nicolas of Flushing [Vlissengen], arrived in London on 11 November 1567 from Flushing. [TNA.E190.4.2]

ANGLO-DUTCH LINKS, 1560-1860

MILNER, JOSEPH, a merchant, and his wife Ann Goodenough, on the north side of Newhaven, Rotterdam, died in Hull, Yorkshire, probate, 1700, PCC

MINNIX, CORNELIUS, GILES MINNIX and LEWES VAN DER GEYNSE, merchants of Middelburg and Flushing, [Vlissengen]; to be reimbursed for cargo taken by Captain Frank and others, May 1589. [Cal.SPForeign.iv.99]

MISSELDEN, EDWARD, in Delft, a letter, 25 June 1625. [SP.Col.1625.78]

MOCATA, MOSES, a merchant in London, later in Amsterdam, probate, 1693, PCC

MOENS, ANN, born in Antwerp, [Antwerpen], a maid in London, probate, 1623, PCC

MOLINEUX, RICHARD, was granted a pass to go to Flanders on 6 June 1685. [SPDom]

MOONE, CLEYS PETER, master of the Michell of Amsterdam arrived in London on 7 October 1567 from Amsterdam. [TNA.E190.4.2]

MOORE, WILLIAM, of Henley Castle, Worcestershire, died in Flanders, probate, 1682, PCC

MORRIS, LEWIS, in Barbados from 1651 to 1689. [TNA.HCA.76. Barclay versus Morris, February 1669]

MORRISON, ROBERT, from Bristol, died in Rotterdam, probate, 1694, PCC

MORTIMER, Mrs MARY, with her servant, were granted a pass to go to Flanders on 30 November 1687. [SPDom]

MOUCHERON, PETER, and MICHAEL LEMAN, Agents for the merchants of Holland and Zeeland, to compensate for the cargoes of two Dutch ships the Fortune and the Dolphin looted by Henry Lewknor, captain of the Peregrine, June 1594. [SPForeign.iv.100]

MOUNTACK, ANDREW, from Barbados aboard the Eliza, master Alexander Mattison, bound for Holland on 16 September 1679. [TNA]

MYNNTULY, ALEXANDER, a merchant from Liege, [Luik], died in London, probate, 1574, PCC

NAVAR, MARGARETA, was granted a pass to go to Holland on 24 April 1690. [SPDom.1690.565]

NEWCOMEN, MATTHEW, born 1610 in Colchester, son of Stephen Newcomen, was educated at the University of Cambridge, BA in 1629, MA in 1633, a leader of the church reform party in Essex, minister in Dedham until 1662, then minister of the Scots Church in Leiden from 1662 until his death on 1 September 1669. Husband of Hannah Snelling, parents of Stephen 1645, Hannah 1647, Martha 1651, Alice 1652, Sarah 1655. [F.7.546]

NICHOLAS, JOHN, a master surgeon from Bordeaux, France, later of Montpelliers Temple, Bloetstraat, Amsterdam, probate, 1695, PCC

NIEREN, JASPER, pastor of the Low Dutch church in Sandwich, died beyond the seas, probate, 1655, PCC

NOLET, ARNOLD ADRIAN, from the Netherlands, residing in London, was naturalised on 10 December 1886. [TNA.HO.334.14.5088]

NORWOOD, WILLIAM, a gentleman from Leckhampton, Gloucestershire, died in Flanders, probate, 1693, PCC

OGLETHORPE, THEOPHILIUS, was commissioned as Colonel of the Holland Regiment in October 1685. [SPDom]

OLIPHANT, CHARLES AGATHON GUILLIAME, from the Netherlands, was naturalised in England on 19 June 1866. [TNA.HO.1.131.5087]

OPPENHEIMER, HERMAN, from the Netherlands, was naturalised in England on 17 June 1872. [TNA.HO.144.434.B28248]

OSBER, MICHAEL, was granted a pass to go to Holland on 24 April 1690. [SPDom.1690.565]

OXENBRIDGE, BATHSUA, daughter of John Oxenbridge an Englishman settled in Boston, married ...... Scott, a planter in Surinam, moved from there via Barbados to New York in 1668, later in Jamaica. [TNA.CO1.31/75]

OUSLEY, CHRISTOPHER, from Dorset, died in Amsterdam, probate, 1688, PCC

OVERS, GRIETIE, a Dutchwoman with children, was granted a pass to go to Holland on 25 April 1690. [SPDom.1690.566]

PAGE, Mrs ANNE, wife of Robert Page, licensed to go to Rotterdam in 1637. [TNA]

ANGLO-DUTCH LINKS, 1560-1860

PAGET, JOHN, Rector of Nantwich, Cheshire in 1598, ejected as a Puritan, fled to Holland, chaplain to the English troops in the service of the States General, minister of the English Reformed Church in Amsterdam from 1607, died 18 August 1638, his son Thomas Paget was minister in Amsterdam from 1639. [F.7.537]

PAGET, NATHAN, born in March 1615 in Manchester, a Puritan, educated at Edinburgh and at Leiden, a physician in London, died in January 1679

PAGET, Reverend ROBERT, born 1612, minister of the English church in Dordrecht, collegiate minister of the Reformed Church in Amsterdam from 1639 to 1646, returned to England, Presbyterian minister of Stockport, Cheshire, died 1684, probate, 1685, PCC, [F.7.538/543]

PAGET, THOMAS, educated at Cambridge University, minister of the English Reformed Church in Amsterdam 1630s, died in Stockport in 1660.

PAIN, HENRY, and his servants, were granted a pass to go to Flanders and return on 5 October 1687. [SPDom]

PALMER, MATHEW, from London, an army captain serving in Flanders, probate, 1692, PCC

PALMER, NICHOLAS, a gentleman and a Captain at Legar Remon in the Low Countries, probate, 1580, PCC

PARDO, JEOSUAH HISQUIAU, was born in Amsterdam in 1626, settled in Curacao from 1647 to 1683, then in Jamaica.

PARISHE, JOYSE, master of the Lamb of Middelburg arrived in Boston, Lincolnshire, from Middelburg on 16 October 1601, returned there on 23 October 1601; also arrived on 4 March 1602 and returned on 24 March 1602. [TNA.E190.393.1]

PARKER, Reverend ROBERT, MA, from Wiltshire, a religious refugee in the Netherlands, husband of Dorothy Stevens, died in July 1614 in Doesburg, Gelderland.

PARKER THOMAS, born 1595 in Stanton St Bernard, Wiltshire, son of Reverend Robert Parker, a Puritan who moved to the Netherlands, then in 1634 to New England aboard Mary and John of London. He settled at Agavan, later in Ipswich, Massachusetts, and finally in Newbury where he died on 24 April 1677.

PARNELL, ROBERT, master of the Mary Catherine of Lee arrived in London on 6 December 1567 from Antwerp, [Antwerpen]. [TNA.E190.4.2]

PATTINSON, W. D., the US Consul in Antwerp, [Antwerpen], died there on 4 July 1836. [GM.ns.6.223]

PAULES, BARTHEL, master of the Anne of Antwerp arrived in London on 7 October 1567 from Antwerp, [Antwerpen], also on 22 December 1567 [TNA.E190.4.2]

PEACH, ARTHUR, born 1615, 'licensed to pass beyond the seas, in 1635, bound for Virginia aboard the Plain Joan, in 1638 he was convicted of murder in Plymouth Colony, died 1638. [HI.27.2/27]

ANGLO-DUTCH LINKS, 1560-1860

PECOCK, WILLIAM, from Feversham, Kent, in Flushing, probate, 1574, PCC

PELLAIN, JEAN, in Amsterdam, a letter urging the English to combine with the Scots at Darien, 1699. [University of London AL.97]

PERCIVALL, ARTHUR, a surgeon from St Botolph, Aldgate, died in Holland, probate, 1694, PCC

PERRY, JONATHAN, from London, died in New Zealand, [in the West Indies?], probate, 1693, PCC

PETERS, BARNARD, master of the Spedegle of Antwerp [Antwerpen], arrived in London on 2 October 1567. [TNA.E190.4.7]

PETERS, HENRY, a sailor in Rotterdam, probate, 1656, PCC

PETERS, JOPE, master of the Lady of Arnemuiden arrived in London on 10 November 1567 from Arnemuiden. [TNA.E190.4.2]

PETERS, NANING, master of the Flower de Luce of Haarlem arrived in London on 11 November 1567. [TNA.E190.4.2]

PETERSON, ALBART, master of the Star of Haarlem arrived in London on 12 November 1567 from Haarlem. [TNA.E190.4.2]

PETERSOUN, CHRISTOPHER, a merchant from Holland, settled in Ireland and was granted denization on 27 January 1662. [BM.ms.Egerton 77]

ANGLO-DUTCH LINKS, 1560-1860

PETERSON, CLAUS, master of the Crown of Amsterdam arrived in Boston, Lincs., on 15 April 1617 from Amsterdam. [TNA.E190. 394.15]

PETERSON, CORNELIUS, a seaman from Amsterdam, died aboard the Josiah, probate, 1700, PCC

PETERSON, DEBUT, master of the Hawk of Muscovy of Amsterdam at Carrickfergus on September 1615. [Temple Newsam mss, West Yorkshire Archives]

PETERSON, JOB, master of the Falcon of Dordrecht arrived in London on 22 December 1567 from Dordrecht. [TNA.E190.4.2]

PETERSON, JOHN, master of the Swan of Flushing [Vlissingen], arrived in London on 25 November 1567. [TNA.E1904.2]

PETERSON, JOHN, a seaman from Amsterdam, died aboard HMS Victory, probate, 1693, PCC

PETERSON, ROSE or RAWSKYN, born in Flanders, a stranger in St Botulph's without Aldgate, London, probate, 1578, PCC

PETERSON, ROWLAND, master of the Paradice of Amsterdam arrived in Boston, Lincs., from Brittany. [TNA.E190. 394.15]

PETERSON, WILLIAM, master of the George of Antwerp, [Antwerpen], arrived in London on 22 November 1567. [TNA.E1904.2]

PEYTON, HENRY, was commissioned as a Captain of the Holland Regiment of Foot on 23 October 1685. [SPDom]

ANGLO-DUTCH LINKS, 1560-1860

PHILIPPART, JACQUES DANIEL, from Belgium, was naturalised in England on 4 June 1868. [TNA.HO1.49.5801]

PICKERING, GILBERT, Thomas Peachey, Robert Coat, and other seamen of the privateer Thomas and Francis, master Gallop, captured the Dutch ship Susannah off the coast of Curacao, on 28 February 1674, sailing from Guinea with a cargo of over 600 Africans and a quantity of gold, a petition regarding that the captain and the Governor of Jamaica kept the whole cargo and did not provide the crew with a share, 6 November 1674. [ActsPCCol.1012]

PICTERNELLE, Miss CORNELIA BROOK, born in Curacao, died 17 July 1826. [Spring Path gravestone, Kingston, Jamaica]

PIETERS, MARY, a Dutchwoman with children, was granted a pass to go to Holland on 25 April 1690. [SPDom.1690.566]

PIETERSE, GERRIT, was granted a pass to go to Holland on 24 April 1690. [SPDom.1690.565]

PIPER, ROBERT, a pirate from Hastings, captured a ship of Amsterdam, master John Somiter, on 25 June 1575.

PLUNKETT, ROBERT, a mariner from Shadwell, Stepney, aboard the Arms of Holland, died at sea, probate 1656 PCC

POLEY, Sir J., in Ostend, a letter, 11 January 1594. [SP.Holland.h142/31]

POPENDUCK, ARNOLD, master of the Owl of Antwerp [Antwerpen], arrived in London on 3 December 1567. [TNA.E190.4.2]

POTTEY, MERMAN, of St Martin's Ongar Lane, London, in 's Hertogenbosch, probate, 1574, PCC

POTTS, THOMAS, son of Thomas Potts minister of the Scots Church in Amsterdam, minister in Flushing, [Vlissingen], from 1646 to 1651, minister of the Scots church in Utrecht from 1651 to 1654, minister of the German congregation in Flushing in 1654, minister of the Dutch Reformed Church there in 1655, died in July 1689. Husband of a daughter of Admiral de Ruyter [F.7.555]

POWELL, WILLIAM, huntsman to the Prince of Orange was granted a pass to go to Holland with forty couples of hounds, on 17 June 1685. [SPDom]

POWNSOR, JAMES, master of the Nicholas of Flushing arrived in Boston, Lincolnshire, from Flushing [Vlissingen], on 17 August 1601, returned there on 30 August 1601. [TNA.E190.393.1]

ANGLO-DUTCH LINKS, 1560-1860

POYNTER, WILLIAM, a gentleman from Richmond, Surrey, died in Breda, probate, 1689, PCC

PRIEST, DIGORY, born 1580, a hatter from London, a Separatist, from Leiden aboard the <u>Speedwell</u>, later aboard the <u>Mayflower</u> bound for America in 1620.

PRINZELL, GEORGE, a goldsmith in the parish of St Martin le Grand, London, and a member of the Dutch Church in London, was granted denization in 1583. [BM.Cecil mss.870]

PRYCE, RICHARD, a yeoman from Munkmore, Shropshire, died in Flanders, probate, 1684, PCC

QUICK, JOHN, born in 1636 in Plymouth, educated at Exeter College, Oxford, graduated BA in 1657, ordained on 2 February 1659, minister of Kingsbridge cum Churchstow, in Devon, probably ejected at the Restoration, though excommunicated he continued to preach until 13 December 1663 when he was imprisoned. By 1679 he was in Holland, minister of the Scots Church in Middelburg from 1680 to 1681, returned to England on 22 July 1681, became a Presbyterian minister in Middlesex Court, Bartholemew Close, Smithfield, died on 29 April 1706. [F.7.548]

RANDALL, JOHN, Mr Pooley's servant, to go to the Hague, 20 April 1685. [SPDom]

RASSCHE, CORNELIS, born 17 November 1689, Member of the Council of Demerara, planter of Markey, died 15 May 1726, also his sister Jesabeth Rassche, born 19 June 1694, died 1695, and his brother Johannes Rassche, born 18 January 1692, died in 1696. [Coomacha Plantation MI, Demerara]

ANGLO-DUTCH LINKS, 1560-1860

RAULINS, JAMES, from Hackney, London, died in Utrecht, probate, 1678, PCC

REINERSON, TERRICK, master of the Fortune of Stavoren, 1629. [THT.328]

RANSBURG, HENRY, from the Netherlands, was naturalised in England on 28 November 1865. [TNA.HO.1.126.4884]

REDE, JOHN, master of the Cloverblade of Amsterdam arrived in London on 8 December 1567. [TNA.E190.4.2]

REVELL, JOHN, master of the Post of Boston arrived in Boston, Lincs., on 10 October 1634 from Rotterdam, from Boston to Calais on10 November 1634, also, arrived on 20 December 1634. [TNA.E190.393.1]

REYGERS, JAN, master of the De Jonge Jan en Theodore, when bound from Surinam to Amsterdam, was captured by HMS Hyena, Captain Edward Thompson, and condemned at the Admiralty Court in Barbados on 17 May 1782. [PC.Col.V.461]

RICHARDSON, EDWARD, minister at Delft in 1643, later in Ripon, Yorkshire, until 1660, a minister in Haarlem, Holland, from 1665-1670, minister of the Scots Church in Leiden from 1670 to 1674, died in Amsterdam around 1677. [F.7.547]

RICKHAM, or SMITH, WILLIAM, a resident of Ostend, [Oostende] died on board the frigate Rose, Commander Robert Nash, in Banda Bay, probate, 1656, PCC

RINDISBACHER, PETER, from Dordrecht, aboard the Wellington, master J. S. Falbister, bound for Hudson Bay to settle at the Red River, Canada, in 1821. [HBRS]

ROBE, WILLIAM, master of the Seawolf of Amsterdam arrived in London on 13 October 1567 from Amsterdam. [TNA.E190.4.2]

ROBERTSON, Major JOHN, Secretary to the government of Curacao, 1808. [BM. Windham Add.37889, ff43-45]

ROBETHON, DANIEL, a merchant in Amsterdam, probate, 1694, PCC

ROBIN, JASPER, a merchant in Amsterdam, a creditor of Josias le Marchand of Guernsey, November 1630. [ActsPC.2.40/362]

ROBINSON, JOHN, born 1576 in Sturton le Steeple, Nottinghamshire, educated at the University of Cambridge, an Anglican priest turned Puritan, minister at St Andrew's, Norwich moved to the Netherlands in 1607, a student at the University of Leiden in 1615, died in Leiden on 1 March 1625, buried in the Pieterskerk. [misc]

ROBINSON, JOHN, born 1615, a tailor from Rye in Suffolk, licensed to go to Rotterdam in 1637. [TNA]

ROBINSON, ROBERT, master of the .... of Sandwich, when bound from Vlissingen, [Flushing], was captured by privateers from Dunkirk in 1624. [ActsPC.V.239]

ROBINSON, ROBERT, master of the Violet of Boston arrived in Boston, Lincs., on 30 September 1634 from Amsterdam. [TNA.E190.393.1]

ROBSON, PETER, master of the Heare of Lee arrived in London on 22 December 1567 from Antwerp. [Antwerpen] [TNA.E190.4.2]

ROGERS, FRANCIS, Michael le Fort and others of Middelburg and Flushing, were commissioned to return the Fortune of Amsterdam with its cargo of Canary wine taken by Edward Lewes, captain of the White Hind of Weymouth and brought to Mount's Bay in England, December 1591. [SPForeign.iv.100]

ROGERSON, JOHN, a merchant from Rotterdam, was granted denization in Ireland on 15 April 1671. [BM.Egerton.1720]

ROHNER, GEORGE WILLIAM, from the Netherlands, was naturalised in England on 11 June 1857. [TNA.HO.1.80.2457]

ROOTH, FRANCIS, from Wexford, Ireland, died in Louvain, [Leuven], Brabant, probate, 1692, PCC

ROVERSON, CLEYS, master of the Unicorn of Haarlem arrived in London on 17 October 1567 from Arnemuiden. [TNA.E190.4.2]

RULICE, JOHN, from London, minister of the Reformed Church in Amsterdam from 1636 to 1637. [F.7.537]

RUSH, NICHOLAS, a clerk in St Anthony's Polder, Holland, probate, 1628, PCC

RUTGERSON, HENRY HUDD, merchant in Amsterdam, to be refunded the cargo stayed aboard the Hope of Hamburg at Dover, England, April 1589. [Cal.SP.Foreign. iv.99]

RUTTER, JOHN, of Rotterdam, owner and master of the Salamon wrecked near Dartmouth, England, a commission March 1590. [SPForeign.iv.99]

RUYTINCTE, MARY, widow of Simon Ruytincte preacher in the Dutch Church in London, probate, 1622, PCC

SALLE, JOHN, a brasier, born in Flanders, settled in Whitechapel, London, probate, 1622; his widow, Agnes Salle, probate, 1625, PCC

SALOMONSON, JOHAN LOUIS, from the Netherlands, resident in Loughton, was naturalised on 20 September 1898. [TNA.HO334.16.5897]

SAMUEL, SAMUEL, born 1752, a clothesman from London, bound via London aboard the Princess Royal for Friesland or employment in March 1774. [TNA.T47.9/11]

SAVARY, ISABELLA, a widow, and her three children, were permitted to go to The Hague, [Den Haag], in April 1631. [ActsPC.2.40/916]

SCHOTT, JACOB, from the Netherlands, was naturalised in England in 1866. [TNA.HO.1.129.4988]

SCORRIER, AUGUSTE, from Belgium, was naturalised in England on 9 May 1862. [TNA.HO1.105.3811]

SCOTT, THOMAS, rector of St Saviour's, Norwich, and minister of St Clement's, Ipswich, fled to Holland, chaplain of the English garrison at Gorcum, minister of the Scots Church in Utrecht in 1622, was assassinated in 1626. [F.7.554]

SEAGON, JOHN, master of the Seagreen of Lynn arrived in Boston, Lincs., on 16 June 1634 from Amsterdam, returned to Amsterdam on 23 May 1634, also, arrived on 28 August 1634, and on 3 November 1634. [TNA.E190.393.1]

SEAVER, ROBERT, son of Thomas Seaver a waterman in London deceased, and an apprentice to Pearte a silk-weaver in Aldgate, London, deceased, on shipboard was impressed for Her Majesty's Service in the Low Countries, probate, 1607, PCC

SEGERS, JOHN, born 1645 in Delfhaven, Rotterdam, settled in St Mary's parish, Whitechapel, London in 1679, foremastman aboard the Anne and Mary bound from London to Virginia in 1690. [TNA.HCA.79]

SEMALL, PETER, born in Bergen, Henegowe, in Newington beyond Southwark, London, probate, 1577. PCC

SENESCHALL, ABRAHAM, born in Antwerp, [Antwerpen], a 'twister of cruell' in Cripplegate, London, probate, 1613, PCC

SENSEN, DANIEL, master of the Cub of Veere arrived in Boston, Lincs., from Veere on 20 January 1634, returned to Veere on 7 February 1634. [TNA.E190.393.1]

SEWELL, SIMOND, born 1607, from Carlton Rod in Norfolk, was licensed to go to Holland in 1637. [TNA]

SENSARFE, GERALD, a mariner from Rotterdam, settled in Ireland and was granted denization on 9 January 1663. [BM.ms.Egerton 77]

SERES, PETER, born in Antwerp, [Antwerpen], Brabant, a merchant in St Botolph, Billingsgate, London, probate, 1583, PCC

SERFATTY, JOSHUA, from Barbados aboard the Morning Star, master John Van Der Spike, bound for Surinam on 29 May 1679. [TNA]

SEYMOUR, Lord GEORGE, naval officer in Curacao, letter, 1803. [Buckinghamshire Record Office, D/MH.M.140]

SHAW, GEORGE, in Antwerp, [Antwerpen], probate, 1690, PCC

SHELSWELL, JOHN, a soldier from London, at Bruges, [Brugge] probate, 1679, PCC

SHENTON, EDWARD, from Clerkenwell, London, in Ghent, [Gent], probate, 1690, PCC

SHEPPARD, RICHARD, in Antwerp, [Antwerpen], probate, 1653, PCC

SIBSEY, SIMON, master of the Susan of Boston from Boston, Lincs., bound for Rotterdam on 13 January 1634. [TNA.E190.393.1]

SIMONDS, WOLF, from the Netherlands, was naturalised in England on 11 June 1862. [TNA.HO.1.105.3840]

SIMONSON, MOSES, emigrated from England or Holland aboard the Fortune, arrived at New Plymouth on 11 November 1621. [NWI.1.15]

SIMONSON, WALTER, master of the Mearman of Haarlem arrived in London on 12 November 1567 from Haarlem. [TNA.E190.4.2]

SIMSON, MARTIN, a widower in Dirckieflips, Somersdyke, Zealand, probate 1696, PCC

SIMPSON, ROWLAND, an English subject and a planter in Surinam, on the colony being returned to the Dutch, sold his plantation, and with his wife and family, along with his 309 hogsheads of sugar, left Surinam aboard the Golden Lyon of Sordam, master Burgh Jacobs, in 1674, bound for Amsterdam, intending to return to England however the ship was captured by a French privateer The Golden Fleece, master Bernard Le Moine near the Scilly Isles and taken to Milford Haven, a petition 11 August 1676. [ActsPCCol.1093]

SLANEY, EDMUND, Keeper of the English Staple at Bruges, [Brugge] died in Brabant, probate, 1578, PCC

SMITH, CHARLES, a merchant in Curacao, died in Portsmouth, England, on 16 September 1809. [GM.79.894]

SMITH, DANIEL, a merchant in Amsterdam, probate, 1679, PCC

SMITH, JOHN, a merchant from Battersea, London, died in Utrecht, probate, 1684, PCC

SMITH, alias RICKHAM, WILLIAM, in Ostend, [Oostende] aboard the frigate Rose, master Robert Nash, in Banda Bay, probate 1656, PCC

SMYTER, REINER EDWARD, from the Netherlands, was naturalised in England on 21 January 1899. [TNA.HO144.434.B28.248]

SOEST, JAMES, in Duke's Place, London, then in Leiden, probate, 1575, PCC

SOLOMAN, JOSEPH, born 1755 a clothesman from London, bound via London aboard the Princess Royal for Friesland and employment in March 1774. [TNA.T47.9/11

SPANGE, WILLIAM, surgeon aboard the man-o-war Le Broke from Veere moored at Gravesend, indicted for the murder of John Johnson a Dutch smith, found guilty, 1675. [Cal. Kent Assizes]

SPARROWHAWK, J., in Ostend, a letter, 4 January 1594. [TNA.SP.Holland.h131/10]

ANGLO-DUTCH LINKS, 1560-1860

SPIERNICK, CORNELIUS, born in Antwerp, [Antwerpen], a doctor of physic, in the city of London, probate, 1578, PCC

SPRITE, CORNILIS JOHNSON, master of the Andrew of Antwerp [Antwerpen], arrived in London on 21 October 1567. [TNA.E190.4.2]

SPROUCK, MARGARET, spouse of Wessel Boshof, in the Hague, [Den Haag], probate, 1699, PCC

STACEY, JOHN, in Brussels, probate, 1692, PCC

STAEL, TETIE, a Dutch woman, was granted a pass to go to Holland on 25 April 1690. [SPDom.1690.566]

STEELE, JOHN, of London, died in Zeeland on his return from Virginia, probate, 1638, PCC

STEWARD, JACOB, master of the Grace of God of Amsterdam arrived in London on 27 November 1567 from Antwerp. [Antwerpen] [TNA.E1904.2]

STIBBE, GODFREY, from the Netherlands, residing in Dunbarton, was naturalised in 1896. [TNA.HO334.24.9040]

STILES, ROBERT, apprentice to Richard Cooke a draper in London, died in Amsterdam, probate, 1680, PCC

STODART, WILLIAM, minister of Rope Walk Chapel in Sunderland, minister of the Scots Church in Amsterdam from 1803 to 1807, emigrated to America, died in Scotland in 1812. [F.7.539]

STOGDELL, JAMES, from Covent Garden, London, died in Flanders, probate, 1693, PCC

ANGLO-DUTCH LINKS, 1560-1860

STOREY, JAMES, servant to Henry Sidney, was granted a pass to go to Holland on 10 August 1687. [SPDom]

STOWE, JOHN, born 1613, from Flushing, [Vlissinggen], Zealand, settled in Bermuda, lodging in Stepney, London, in 1669. [TNA.HCA.76. Barkely versus Morris]

STUCLINCKE, DIGNA, wife of Reynier Cuenans of Billeter Lane, London, probate, 1574, PCC

STURTIVANT, JOHN, a merchant in London trading with Antwerp [Antwerpen], in 1567. [TNA.E190.4.2]

SWAAB, SAMUEL LEON, from the Netherlands, was naturalised in England on 9 July 1861. [TNA.HO.1.3591]

SWABE, DAVID, from Belgium, naturalised in England on 21 November 1856. [TNA.HO1.78.2362]

SWAN, JOHN, master of the Hope of Amsterdam was buried in St Michael's, Barbados, on 26 March 1678. [HOT.425]

SWARTE, PETER HENDRICKSON, master of the Jonas of Amsterdam with cargo, stayed at Dungarven, Ireland, by Charles Walcot, April 1592. [SPForeign.iv.100]

SYMS, WILLIAM, master of the Barsaby of Lee arrived in London on 11 December 1567 from Antwerp, [Antwerpen] [TNA.E190.4.2]

SYVERSSON, JOHN, born in Amsterdam, a merchant stranger in Woolwich, Kent, probate, 1581, PCC

ANGLO-DUTCH LINKS, 1560-1860

TAYSPILL, JOHN, a widower and a merchant in Amsterdam, probate, 1680, PCC

TERMA, MARGRIET, a Dutchwoman with children, was granted a pass to go to Holland on 25 April 1690. [SPDom.1690.566]

TERRY, EDWARD, in Utrecht, serving in the wars of the Low Countries, probate, 1627, PCC

THAYER, JOHN, a miner in Captain John Firs company, died in Flanders On His Majesty's Service, probate 1694, PCC

THIERRY, JAMES, a merchant in Amsterdam, died in Holland, probate 1698, PCC

THOMPSON, ANNE, born 1577, wife of John Thompson in Yarmouth, and their daughter Bridget, licensed to go to Rotterdam in 1637. [TNA]

THORPE, JOHN, master of the Sea Venture of Boston arrived in Boston, Lincs., on 7 June 1634 from Amsterdam. [TNA.E190.393.1]

TINNE, ADRIEN ABRAHAM ALEXANDER, born 28 July 1785, Assistant to the Court of Justice and Policy in Demerara, died 21 August 1815. [Bourda gravestone, Vlissingen, Demerara]

TORIUS, JOHN, a Flemish physician in London, probate, 1572, PCC

TREVOR, ROBERT, born 1706, died 1783, Secretary of the British Legation at the Hague, 1734-1739, and Envoy to the States General from 1739 to 1746, papers. [Buckinghamshire Record Office]

TROOSTWYK, BENEDICTUS, from the Netherlands, was naturalised in England on 15 October 1869. [TNA.HO.1.159.6339]

TRYOEN, PETER, born in Wulnergem in Flanders, a free denizen of England, in London, probate, 1611, PCC

TWIDEN, HENEAGE, aboard the Dutch ship Pastime, master Nico Marredelt, died in London, probate, 1680, PCC

TYMBREMAN, MAURICE, a merchant in London trading with Danzig in 1567. [TNA.E190.4.2]

TYNDALE, ARTHUR, a citizen and mercer of London, and a merchant adventurer of England, now in Delft, probate, 1625, PCC

TYSER, JACOB, master of the Swan of Amsterdam arrived in London from Amsterdam in 1567 with a cargo for Edward Van Crog. [TNA.E190.4.2]

TYSON, JACOB, master of the Longbow of Amsterdam arrived in London on 17 November 1567 from Amsterdam. [TNA.E190.4.2]

UDALL, Sir E., in Flushing, [Vlissingen], 7 January 1594. [SP.Holland.h135/18]

ULRICK, alias FALCONIER, Captain, master of the Dutch privateer Mount Aetna captured the brigantine Isaac bound from Barbados, 1695. [ActsPCCol.608]

UNDERWOOD, ALWORTH, a yeoman from Northamptonshire, died in Flanders, probate, 1693, PCC

VALKAERT, DENNIS, of St Benet Sherhogg, a Dutch Church in London, probate 1581, PCC

VALLINE, JOHN, born in Ryssell, Flanders, a clockmaker in London, probate, 1605, PCC

VAN ADENA, EDWARD, a merchant in London trading with Dordrecht in 1567. [TNA.E190.4.2]

VAN ADINEK, MELCHIOR, a merchant in London trading with Dordrecht in 1567. [TNA,190.4.2]

VAN AECKERLEN, HELEN, widow of Jodocus Faes of Antwerp, [Antwerpen], died in Middleborough, probate, 1574, PCC

VAN ALDEN, GAWEN, a merchant in London trading with Dordrecht in 1567. [TNA.E190.4.2]

VAN AMSTEL, SARAH, a resident of the parish of All Hallows, London, 1695. [CLRO]

VAN ANWEGHEM, JOHN, of St George Botolph Lane, London, probate, 1574, PCC

VAN ASSE, MELCHIOR, born in Geldermalisson, in the country of Gelderland, in St Nicholas, London, probate, 1582, PCC

VAN BAG, CORNELIA, a Dutch woman, was granted a pass to go to Holland on 25 April 1690. [SPDom.1690.566]

VAN BEELEN, JOHN, died in St Elizabeth's, Jamaica, on 15 August 1793. [GM.63.1051]

VAN BELLE, PETER, a denizen and planter on St Kitts, petitioned the Privy Council Colonial on 9 March 1704.

VAN BEMMEL, MARGARET, was buried in the chancel of St Katherine by the Tower, London, on 5 January 1684.

VAN BEMMELL, THOMAS, was buried in the chancel of St Katherine by the Tower on 18 February 1685.

VAN BERCHIN, HENRY, residing in the parish of St Christopher le Stocks, London, 1695. [CLRO]

VAN BERRINBROOK, PHILIP, the King's falconer in 1685. [SPDom]

VAN BREDA, JOHANNES, from the Netherlands, was granted naturalisation in 1865. [TNA.HO.1.120.4676]

VAN BROKE, PETER, with Elizabeth his wife, residing in Foster Lane, St Leonard, London, 1695. [CLRO]

VAN BROOKE, CARLETON, a servant, residing in the parish of All Hallows the Less, London, 1695. [CLRO]

VAN BROOKE, DUDLEY, was commissioned as an Ensign in Captain Weld's company on 21 September 1688. [SPDom]

VAN BRUGHEN, GOMERD, in London, probate, 1570, PCC

VAN BRUSSINGHAM, SEBASTIAN, residing in the parish of St Andrew Hubbard, London, 1695. [CLRO]

VAN BUCKHOVEN, General Major PHILLIPPUS ALBERTUS, petitioned for payment of a pension promised in 1669 when he settled in England after he served in Russia, [SPDom.1670.630]

VAN CAMP, GERARDUS FRANCIS, from Belgium, was naturalised in England on 11 May 1870.
[TNA.HO1.162.6456]

ANGLO-DUTCH LINKS, 1560-1860

VAN CARCO, JACOB, was buried in the Flemish yard of St Katherine by the Tower, London, on 12 August 1686.

VAN CASTER, ENGEN, daughter of Otto and Jane Van Caster, was baptised in St Katherine by the Tower, London, on 8 February 1691.   0

VAN CASTER, INGOR, daughter of Otto and Jane Van Caster, was baptised in St Katherine by the Tower, London, on 14 February 1692.

VAN CASTER, INGOR, daughter of Otto and Jane Van Caster, was baptised in St Katherine by the Tower, London, on 24 May 1694.

VAN CASTER, MARTIN, son of Otto and Jane Van Caster, was baptised in St Katherine by the Tower, London, on 23 January 1696.

VAN COLLEN, HARMAN, a brewer in St Olave, Southwark, Surrey, probate, 1570, PCC

VAN COULSTERS, DANIEL, was commissioned as an Ensign in Sir Edward Hale's company on 21 September 1688. [SPDom]

VAN CROG, EDWARD, a merchant in London trading with Antwerp [Antwerpen], and Hamburg in 1567. [TNA.E190.4.2]

VAN DACHELOR, JOHN, wife Mary, son Daniel, and daughter Susan, residing in the parish of St Mary Bothaw, London, 1695. [CLRO]

VAN DALE, JOHN, a merchant in London, probate, 1606, PCC

VAN DALEN, LYSBETT, with children, was granted a pass to go to Holland on 25 April 1690. [SPDom.1690.566]

VAN DAMME, WILLIAM, born in Ghent, [Gent], a thread-dyer in London, probate, 1625, PCC

VAN DAN, JOHN, residing in the parish of St Anne Blackfriars, London, 1695. [CLRO]

VAN DANAKER, MARTIN, and his wife Mary, residing in the parish of St James Garlickhithe, London, 1695. [CLRO]

VAN DEANCHER, ROBERT, a servant, residing in the parish of St Bartholomew by the Exchange, London, 1695. [CLRO]

VAN DECKEELL, HUBBARD, in Southwark, probate, 1612, PCC

VAN DE LURE, JAMES, from Middelburg, Zealand, settled in Cork, Ireland and granted denization on 1 September 1663. [BM.ms.Egerton 77]

VANDEL-VANDEN, FRANCIS, son of Abraham Vandel-Vanden, was baptised in St Katherine by the Tower, London, on 30 May 1694.

VAN DENANCOR, MARTIN, an apprentice, residing in the parish of St Mary le Bow, London, 1695. [CLRO]

VAN DENANCOR, MARY, a servant, residing in the parish of St Katherine Cree, London, in 1695. [CLRO]

VAN DEPERE, M., a correspondent in Nieuport, Flanders, in 1672. [SP.Dom.1672.275]

ANGLO-DUTCH LINKS, 1560-1860

VAN DEPOL, ADAM, son of John Van Depol, was baptised in St Katherine by the Tower, London, on 18 May 1676.

VAN DE POOLE, JAMES, in St Ethelburgh, London, probate, 1605, PCC

VAN DE WATER, SIBERT, a cooper from Dordrecht in Holland, settled in Ireland and was granted denization on 27 February 1662. [BM.ms. Egerton 77]

VAN DEN ANKER, PETER, a merchant, was granted a patent on 7 August 1687. [SPDom]

VAN DENBEND, JOHN, with his wife Catherine, sons Thomas and Elishimon, and daughter Elizabeth, residing in the parish of Allhallows the Great, London, in 1695. [CLRO]

VAN DEN BERGH, ELIZABETH, widow of Theodorus van der Bergh, in Colchester, Essex, probate, 1615, PCC

VAN DEN BOSSCHE, JACQUES, from Drynse in Flanders, then in Maidstone, Kent, probate, 1621, PCC

VAN DEN BURGH, TOBIAS, a servant, residing in the parish of St Martin Orgar, London, in 1695. [CLRO]

VAN DEN BURGH, WILLIAM, with William Van Den Burgh junior, residing in the parish of St Martin Orgar, London, in 1695. [CLRO]

VAN DEN BURGH, ..., residing in the parish of St Ethelburga, London, in 1695. [CLRO]

VAN DEN BUSCH, JASPER, with wife Ann, daughters Annamarie, Susan, Angoneto, Elizabeth, and Mary, son

Jasper, residing in the parish of All Hallows the Less, London, in 1695. [CLRO]

VAN DEN POLE, JOHN, in All Hallows, Lombard Street, London, probate, 1581, PCC

VAN DE POST, ADRIAN, with wife Mary, residing in the parish of St Mary at Hill, London, in 1695. [CLRO]

VAN DER BEECKE, ALEXANDER, was granted a pass to go to Holland on 24 April 1690. [SPDom.1690.565]

VAN DER CLUSE, ANNA, was buried in the Flemish yard of St Katherine by the Tower, London, on 2 August 1678.

VAN DER CLUSE, EDWARD, son of John Van Der Cluse, was baptised in St Katherine by the Tower, London, on 3 October 1680.

VAN DER CLUSE, JOHN, was buried in the Flemish yard of St Katherine by the Tower, London, on 29 July 1678

VAN DER CLUSE, MARY, was buried in the Flemish yard of St Katherine by the Tower, London, on 10 August 1678

VAN DERER, DANIEL, a servant, residing in the parish of St Mary Colechurch, London, in 1695. [CLRO]

VAN DER ELST, MARGARET, widow of John Coen, born in Menin, Flanders, later in London, probate, 1575, PCC

VAN DER ESPT, or CARBONELL, ABIGAIL, a widow in London, probate, 1608, PCC

ANGLO-DUTCH LINKS, 1560-1860

VAN DER FORD, ABRAHAM and JOHN, factors in Limerick for John Munsey, a merchant in London, trading with Middelburg, Zeeland, a petition, 23 May 1631. [ActsPC.2.40/1035]

VAN DER HAVEN, JOHN, married Frances Knightley in St Margaret's, Westminster, on 21 October 1679.

VAN DER HEWER, ARNOLD, a juryman at Maidstone Assizes in 1573. [Cal.Kent Assizes]

VAN DER HOLFSTAD, JOHN, in St George's, Botolph Lane, London. probate, 1581, PCC

VAN DER HONNE, SEGEBERTUS, in Christ Church, London, probate, 1579, PCC

VAN DER HOVE, JOHN BAPTISTA, a merchant supplying ships components in 1668. [SPDom.]

VAN DER HURST, ISABELLA, was buried in the Flemish yard of St Katherine by the Tower, London on 9 April 1683.

VAN DER HURST, WILLIAM, was convicted of horse-stealing at the Old Bailey, imprisoned in Newgate, was pardoned on 31 July 1681. [SPDom]

VAN DER LINDE, JOHN, a merchant, died in Curacao on 4 January 1815. [GM.86.473]

VAN DER LURE, PETER, merchant aboard the Fortune of Flushing arrived in Boston, Lincolnshire, from Bordeaux on 2 December 1601; also, on the Nicholas of Flushing from Flushing [Vlissingen], on 17 August 1602; a merchant trading between Rotterdam and Boston in 1634. [TNA.E190.393.1]

VAN DER MARSH, PETER, with John and Agnes Van Der Marsh, residing in the parish of St Martin Orgar, London, in 1695. [CLRO]

VAN DER MINDER, JACOB, a Dutchman, with wife Ellenor, and son William, residing in the parish of St Andrew Undershaft, London, in 1695. [CLRO]

VAN DER MUELEN, STEPHEN, in St Andrew Undershaft, London, probate, 1563, PCC

VAN DER NOTT, AUGUSTINE, probate, 1576, PCC

VAN DERO, JAN, in St Stephen, Colman Street, London, probate, 1583, PCC

VAN DER POEST, JOHN, in Norwich, probate, 1607, PCC

VAN DER POLL, KATHERINE, a servant, residing in the parish of St Anne, Blackfriars, London, in 1695. [CLRO]

VAN DER POOLE, KATHERINE, daughter of Michael and Elizabeth Van Der Poole, was baptised in St Margaret's, Westminster, on 25 August 1678.

VAN DER POOLE, THOMAS, son of Michael and Elizabeth Van Der Poole, was baptised in St Margaret's, Westminster, on 8 March 1677.

VAN DER SNOOKE, CORNELIA, was buried in St Katherine by the Tower, London, on 10 October 1677.

VAN DER SPIKE, master of the <u>Morning Star</u> bound from Barbados to Surinam on 28 My 1679. [HOT.407]

VAN DER STILTE, LYVEN, a Dutch merchant, to be compensated for the cargo of the <u>Bonadventure of Calais</u> taken by John Nicholls who was executed, September 1592. [SPForeign.iv.100]; and Jorine Reiwart alias Busbier his wife, probate, 1609, PCC

VAN DER STELT, LIEVEN, son of Lieven Van Der Stelt in Ghent, [Gent], in Bishopsgate, London, probate, 1608, PCC

VAN DER SPRITT, JOHN, was granted denization on 23 July 1687. [SPDom]

VAN DER SPRETT, JOHN, with his sister Ann, and brother William, residing in the parish of St Benet Fink, London, in 1695. [CLRO]

VAN DER TIN, GERRARD, with wife Mary, and daughter Aletta, residing in the parish of St Martin, Vintry, London, in 1695. [CLRO]

VAN DER VALLYE, HENRY, a baillie discharged at Maidstone, Kent Assizes in 1594. [Cal.Kent Assizes]

VAN DER VELDIN, DOROTHY, with her son Francis, residing in the parish of All Hallows, Barking, London, in 1695. [CLRO]

VAN DER VENDEN, ABRAHAM, was buried in St Dunstan in the East, London, on 16 October 1694.

VAN DER VINCKT, JOHN, born in Ghent, [Gent], later in London, probate, 1607, PCC

VAN DER VOORT, JOHN, in Middeburg, Zealand, with links to Ireland, probate, 1656, PCC

VAN DESTEI, EVERS, was granted a pass to go to Holland on 24 April 1690. [SPDom.1690.565]

VAN DIEGENHEIM, MORRIS, from the Netherlands, was naturalised in England on 9 February 1869. [TNA.HO.1.154.6081]

VAN DIKE, ALLARD, was buried at St Dunstan in the East, London, on 28 June 1723.

VAN DIKE, Sir ANTHONY, in Antwerp, [Antwerpen], probate, 1688, PCC

VAN DIKE, JOHN, of Dunkirk, master of the Mary of Gravelin, a privateer, captured the Hope of Zuricksea, near Scarborough, Yorkshire, and looted the cargo of Archibald Nicholl in Stirling and George Burfield of Newcastle on Tyne on 16 May1624. [Acts.PC.V.238]

VAN DINANDO, ANNE, daughter of Cornelius and Anne Van Dinando, was baptised in St Margaret's, Westminster, on 3 March 1680.

VAN DINANDO, JOHN, son of Cornelius and Ann Van Dinando, was baptised in St Margaret's, Westminster, on 27 November 1677.

VAN DINGHAN, CORNELIS, from Breda, in London, probate, 1570, PCC

VAN DOLHERN, CLAUS, born 1760, died 24 October 1807. [Kingston gravestone, Jamaica]

VAN DORNE, LUDER, a merchant in London trading with Hamburg in 1567. [TNA.E190.4.2]

ANGLO-DUTCH LINKS, 1560-1860

VAN DRAL, J., from Holland, landed in Norwich on 10 June 1811. [TNA.FO.83.21]

VAN DYNGHEN, CORNELIUS, from Breda, in London, probate, 1570, PCC

VAN EITSON, DANIEL, a merchant in London trading with Hamburg and Amsterdam in 1567. [TNA.E190.4.2]

VAN ESSEN, JACOB, from the Netherlands, residing in London, was naturalised in 1894. [TNA.HO334.21.7848]

VAN ESSEN, Dr SAMUEL, was buried in the Green yard of St Katherine by the Tower, London, on 8 August 1682.

VAN GENEW, Mr GERRARD, was buried in St Margaret's, Westminster, on 19 September 1665.

VAN GENNE, JOHN, born in Venlo, Gelderland, a merchant in London, probate, 1656, PCC

VAN GROVESTINE, ….., former Governor General of Demerara, letters, 1795-1800. [NRS.GD46.17.14]

VAN HAACKE, CHRISTIAN WILHELM, Baron of Rochester, an inventor, 3 March 1772. [CalHOpp1772.619]

VAN HAM, MARY, was buried in the church of St Katherine by the Tower, London, on 8 November 1679.

VAN HANGEN, CORNELIA, a widow in Bishopsgate, London, probate, 1618, PCC

VAN HANSWICK, HANS JOHN, a merchant of Antwerp, [Antwerpen], residing in London, probate, 1561, PCC

VAN HASEVELT, DANIEL, born in Rowsoe, Flanders, a merchant in London, probate, 1625, PCC

VAN HATTEN, JOHN, a merchant, with his wife Lydia, son John, and daughter Katherine, residing in the parish of St Mary Bothaw, London, in 1695. [CLRO]

VAN HECK, OLIVER, born 1600, with his wife Katherine born 1601, and son Peter born 1628, emigrated from London aboard the Transport of London master Edward Walker, bound for Virginia on 4 July 1635. [TNA.E157.20]

VAN HECK, PETER, a recusant in Kent in 1685, [SPDom]

VAN HECKE, PETER, born in Antwerp, [Antwerpen], later of Linstead, Kent, probate, 1690, PCC

VAN HEL, FRANCIS NICHOLAS, son of Nicholas and Mary Van Hel, was baptised in St Katherine by the Tower, London, on 22 February 1688.

VAN HEL, WILLIAM, son of Nicholas and Mary Van Hel, was baptised in St Katherine by the Tower, London, on 25 June 1668.

VAN HELMONT, Baron FRANCISCUS MERCURIUS, petitioned Charles II on behalf of Princess Elizabeth, daughter of the King of Bohemia in 1671. [SPDom.1671.56]; to go, with three servants, to Ireland in 1685. [SPDom]

VAN HELPEN, Baron CONDERS, in Groningen Holland, offered to raise 1200 sailors for British service in June 1770. [TNA.HO.pp. 1770.194]

ANGLO-DUTCH LINKS, 1560-1860

VAN HERNPECKH, LEONARD JACOB, a yeoman in Islington, convicted of forgery, was granted a free pardon on 29 April 1772. [TNA.HO pp.1772.617]

VAN HERWICK, STEPHEN, in All Hallows, Barking, probate, 1566, PCC

VAN HIELE, GILES, from Hamme, Grembergen, Flanders, later in St Dennis in Fenchurch, Lime Street, London, probate, 1578, PCC

VAN HILTON, HENRY, a merchant in London, probate, 1615, PCC

VAN HITTERNE, ABIGALL, with sister Deborah, residing in the parish of St Michael, Cornhill, London, in 1695. [CLRO]

VAN HOGARDEN, ABRAHAM, a merchant from Holland, settled in Ireland and was granted denization on 27 January 1662. [BM.ms.Egerton 77]

VAN HOGARDEN, ISAAC, a merchant from Holland, settled in Ireland and was granted denization on 27 January 1662. [BM.ms. Egerton 77]

VAN HOGARDEN, JACOB, a merchant from Holland, settled in Ireland and was granted denization on 27 January 1662. [BM.ms. Egerton 77]

VAN HOGARDEN, PETER, a merchant from Holland, settled in Ireland and was granted denization on 27 January 1662. [BM.ms. Egerton 77]

VAN HOPE, PHILIP, with his daughters Mary and Ann, residing in the parish of St Anne, Blackfriars, London, in 1695. [CLRO]

ANGLO-DUTCH LINKS, 1560-1860

VAN HORE, HOP, wished to have an audience with the Earl of Rochford on 30 September 1772. [TNA.HO pp.1772.1475]

VAN HORNE, or VUYTENHONE, ANN, a widow in London, probate, 1571, PCC

VAN HOVE, FREDERICK, with his wife Audrey, residing in the parish of St Anne, Blackfriars, London, in 1695. [CLRO]

VAN HOVE, JOHN, in the Diocese of London, probate, 1574, PCC

VAN HOVEN, ELIZABETH, a servant, residing in the parish of St Margaret, Lothbury, London, in 1695. [CLRO]

VAN HULSTE, JOHN, in Barking, London, probate, 1606, PCC

VAN HUSELLS, HERTROY, residing in the parish of All Hallows, London Wall, in 1695. [CLRO]

VAN ILE, CECILIA, was buried in Flemish yard of St Katherine by the Tower, London, on 5 December 1692.

VAN ILE, DERRICK BASTIAN, a child, was buried in the Flemish yard of St Katherine by the Tower, London, on 6338 October 1692

VAN ILE, JOHN, son of Sebastian Van Ile, was baptised in St Katherine by the Tower, London, on 7 November 1695.

VAN ITTREN. GODFREY, a servant, residing in the parish of St Gabriel, Fenchurch, London, in 1695. [CLRO]

VAN LANDERKIN, HERMAN, with wife Phellis, son James, daughters Elizabeth and Mary, residing in the parish of All Hallows, London Wall, in 1695. [CLRO]

VAN LANG, RICHARD, was buried on 21 July 1679 in St Michael's, Barbados. [HOT.425]

VAN LASTICK, THOMAS, son of Henry and Elizabeth Van Lastick, was baptised in St Margaret's, Westminster, on 8 February 1680.

VAN LETTREN, GYSBENT, a servant, residing in the parish of All Hallows, Staining, London, in 1695. [CLRO]

VAN LIMBURG, MARY, was buried in the Flemish yard of St Katherine by the Tower, London, on 17 April 1690.

VAN LITH, HENRICK, a merchant from Dordrecht in Holland, settled in Ireland and was granted denization on 17 February 1667. [BM.ms.Egerton 77]

VAN LUCCOM, HENRY, born 1614, emigrated from England to Barbados aboard the Falcon in December 1635. [TNA.E157.20]

VAN LUENEN, alias SADELA, PETER, ordinary post of Antwerp, [Antwerpen], later in London, probate, 1609, PCC

VAN MATTEVOORTE, FREDRICK, a juryman at Rochester Assizes in 1586. [Cal.Kent Assizes]

VAN NECK, Sir JOSHUA, agent of the French Court in England in 1771. [HO pp.650]

VAN NIER, ROBERT, an indentured servant bound from Bristol to Virginia in August 1658. [BRO]

VAN OMAN, JOHN, was buried in the Flemish yard of St Katherine by the Tower, London, on 4 September 1680.

VAN OME, JOHN, residing in the parish of St Mary, Woolnoth, London, in 1695. [CLRO]

VAN OYE, CORNELIUS, master of a Dutch pinnace of war, was driven into Plymouth with three prize Spanish ships, but was forcibly detained there in September 1630, a petition. [ActsPC.2.40/194]

VAN PAYNE, ISAAC, an investor in the English East India Company in 1626. [SP.Col.1626.299]

VAN PEENE, LUCAS, in St Lawrence Poultry, London, probate, 1577, PCC

VAN PEEVEN, LUKE, born 1596 in London, son of Luke Peeven, probate, 1615, PCC

VAN PHRAN, Colonel of the Dutch at the Cape of Good Hope provided intelligence about the French garrison in Mauritius, 1771. [TNA.HO pp.1771.774.

VAN RAALE, JOEL, from the Netherlands, was naturalised in England in 1867. [TNA.HO.1.139.5394]

VAN RAALE, LION, from the Netherlands, was naturalised in England on 16 March 1867. [TNA.HO.1.139.5393]

VAN RAALE, SALOMON, from the Netherlands, was naturalised in England on 16 March 1867. [TNA.HO.1.139.5395]

VAN REID, HENRY, nephew of Captain Adrian Van Reid, and son of Captain Henry Van Reid, petitioned to be released from prison in Colchester on 25 July 1665. [SPDom]

VAN RENSELAER, NICHOLAS, was appointed as minister of the Dutch congregation in London on 31 March 1668. [Cal.SPDom]

VAN RETI, HENDRICK, born in Goch in the Duchy of Cleve, dwelling in London, probate, 1614, PCC

VAN ROKEGHEM, REMEUS, a merchant in Norwich, probate, 1619, PCC

VAN RUVEN, THEODORE, and his wife, secretary to the Prince of Orange, an associate of Charles II when in the Netherlands, settled in England after the Restoration of the Monarchy, petitioned for the Dutch prize ship then at Limehouse, 1670. [SPDom.1670]

VAN RUYDEN, DERRICK, son of Derrick and Mary Van Ruyden, was baptised in St Dunstan in the East, London, on 22 February 1698.

VAN RUYDEN, HENRY, son of Derrick and Mary Van Ruyden, was baptised in St Dunstan in the East, London, on 10 December 1700.

VAN SCHUYLEN BURCH, PAULUS, Commodore of Demerara, negotiated with Governor Cunninghame of Barbados re the capitulation of Demerara in February 1781. [Acts.PC.Col.1781.1006]

VAN SERGOUDO, TERENIS PIETERSE, was granted a pass to go to Holland on 24 April 1690. [SPDom.1690.565]

VAN SITTER, MARY, a widow, residing in the parish of St Michael, Cornhill, London, in1695. [CLRO]

VAN SITTERN, PETER, with wife Susan, sons Robert, Peter, and William, daughter Susan, residing in the parish of St Andrew Undershaft, London, in 1695. [CLRO]

VAN SLOT, JACOB LAUWER, master of the White Angel from the Capes of Virginia bound for Amsterdam on 6 June 1659. [CLRO]

VAN SON, LYSBET, a Dutch woman, was granted a pass to go to Holland on 25 April 1690. [SPDom.1690.566],

VAN SPEYBROOKE, JOHN, born in Nevelle, Flanders, now in Maidstone, Kent, probate, 1576, PCC

VAN SPRECLESON, HARTIK, a merchant in London trading with Antwerp [Antwerpen] in 1567. [TNA.E190.4.2]

VAN SUNDER, MARY, daughter of William and Elizabeth Van Sunder, was baptised in St Margaret's, Westminster, on 2 February 1680.

VAN TASSENBEECK, FRANCOIS, was granted a pass to go to Holland on 24 April 1690. [SPDom.1690.565]

VAN TEYLINGEN, CHRISTIAN, formerly Governor of the Dutch settlements in the East Indies, took refuge in England having defrauded the Dutch East India Company, sought by Count Welderen, the Envoy Extraordinary of the States General on 7 March 1772. [HO pp.1144]

VAN TRILL, PETER, of Amsterdam, a commission for the restitution of the cargo of the Joshua and of the Sampson taken by the Earl of Cumberland, April 1592. [SPForeign.iv.100]

VAN VLIET, EDWARD, from the Netherlands, was naturalised in England on 1 February 1864. [TNA.HO.1.113.4278]

VAN WACHTENDONKE, JOHN, Commissary of the United Provinces, and William Freeman, agent for Colonel Stapleton, a petition concerning the right of negros taken off Tobago by the ketch Quaker, 16 April 1679. [ActsPCCol]

VAN WALEVELT, GERRITT JANSE DE RIDDER, died aboard the ship William and Richard when bound from St Helena to England, probate, 1700, PCC

VAN WESTERBRUGGE, CORNELIA, daughter of John Westerbrugge, was baptised in St Katherine by the Tower, London, on 1 March 1682.

VAN WYCKEWOORT, JOHN, was granted denization in England on 30 June 1670. [SPDom.1670]

VANE, Sir WALTER, LATE Colonel of the Holland Regiment of Foot, 1773. [SP.Dom]

VER BEKE, MARIE, widow of Nicholas Ver Beck, in Norwich, probate, 1607, PCC

VER BEYST, JOSEPH, from Belgium, was naturalised in England on 14 September 1864. [TNA. HO1.117.4495]

VER BROEGHE, JOHN, a will in Dutch, Sandwich, 1641, PCC

VER MULEN, HESTER, was buried in the chancel of St Katherine by the Tower, London, on 13 December 1679.

ANGLO-DUTCH LINKS, 1560-1860

VER NATTI, JERAVANA, was buried in St Katherine by the Tower, London, on 23 August 1673.

VER NATTI, PETERNELLA, was buried in St Katherine by the Tower, London, on 27 July 1676.

VER NATTY, SARAH PETRONILLA, was buried in the church of St Katherine by the Tower, London, on 3 October 1679.

VEROLICKHOVEN, DAVID, born in Valkenburg, later in London, probate, 1616, PCC

VER SELLIN, ELIZABETH, widow of Jacob Ver Silyn in London, probate, 1607, PCC

VER SELLIN, JACOB, a free denizen of England, in London, probate, 1607, PCC

VITIBULL, ..., master of a privateer of Dunkirk, attacked and captured the Blessing of Dundee, on 13 May 1623, when bound from Sheraut in France to London, a memorial from the Privy Council of England to Sieur Van Male, agent to the Archduchess at Brussels in 1624. [ActsPC.VI.238]

WAESBERGH, PETER, a merchant from Rotterdam, settled in Ireland and was granted denization on 19 July 1665. [BM.ms.Egerton 77]

WARD, HENRY, born 1618, from Wortwell in Norfolk, licensed to 'serve the States' in 1637. [TNA]

WEBER, CHARLES ALBERT, from Belgium, was naturalised in England on 5 August 1856. [TNA.HO1.74.2288]

ANGLO-DUTCH LINKS, 1560-1860

WEBER, HERMANN DAVID, from Belgium, was naturalised in England on 13 August 1866. [TNA.HO1.133.5160]

WELTER, THOMAS, born 1607, a cordiner in Norwich, licensed to go to Rotterdam in 1637. [TNA]

WEST, ANTHONY, a gentleman in The Hague, [Den Haag], probate, 1689, PCC

WHEELER, THOMAS, a merchant of Great Yarmouth, was granted a passport to go to Holland and return on 17 July 1685. [SPDom]B11898]

WHITE, JOHN, master of the John of Flushing arrived in London on 29 November 1567 from Flushing. [Vlissingen] [TNA.E1904.2]

WHITE, PETER, born 1743, a sugar baker from London, bound via London aboard the Princess Royal for Friesland for employment in March 1774. [TNA.T47.9/11]

WIENER, ISADORE, from the Netherlands, was naturalised in England in 1892. [TNA.HO.144. 336.]

WILHELM, CAREL, from the Netherlands, was naturalised in England on 19 October 1865. [TNA.HO.1.125.4844]

WILKINS, GEORGE, from the Netherlands, was naturalised in England in 1864. [TNA.HO.1.117.4514]

WILLEMS VAN ACHERSLOOT, GERARD, from North Holland, a mariner aboard the England, probate, 1693, PCC

ANGLO-DUTCH LINKS, 1560-1860

WILLEMSTEYN, HENDRIK, a servant of the Prince of Orange, was granted a pass to go to Holland on 13 April 1672. [SPDom.1672.317]

WILLIAMS, JAMES, from Northamptonshire, minister of the English church in Amsterdam, probate, 1680, PCC

WILLIAMS, RICHARD, a gentleman from St Giles-in-the-Fields, London, died in Breda, Brabant, probate, 1697, PCC

WILLIAMS, THOMAS, from Yarmouth, Norfolk, a Separatist, from Leiden aboard the Speedwell, later aboard the Mayflower bound for America in 1620, died 1621.

WILLIAMSON, ADRIAN, master of the Falcon of Bergen-op-Zoom arrived in London on 6 October 1567 from Bergen-op-Zoom; master of the Sampson of Antwerp [Antwerpen], arrived in London on 3 December 1567. [TNA.E190.4.2]

WILLIAMSON, ANTHONY, master of the Falcon of Dordrecht arrived in London on 12 November 1567 from Dordrecht. [TNA.E190.4.2]

WILLIAMSON, DOMINICK, a merchant from Flushing, [Vlissingen], settled in Ireland and was granted denization on 12 October 1669. [BM.ms.Egerton 77]

WILLIAMSON, JAMES, a seaman aboard the Rachel when bound from Newcastle for London, was captured by the Dutch on 24 July 1663 and imprisoned in Ostend. [Oostende] [SPDom.1663.688]

WILLIAMSON, THOMAS, from Harwich to Holland in January 1672. [SPDom.1672.89]

WING, JOHN, a minister in Sandwich, Kent, then chaplain to the Merchant Adventurers of England in Hamburg, minister of

Flushing, [Vlissingen], from 1620 to 1627, then minister of the Scots Church in the Hague from 1627 until his death in 1629. [F.7.545]

WINNOX, JOSHUA, was granted a pass to go to Holland on 21 July 1685. [SPDom]

WINTLE, JOSEPH, a tailor from St Clement Danes, Middlesex, died in Amsterdam, probate, 1684, PCC

WITTSZOON, CORNELIS JACQUES, a burgher of Amsterdam, co-owner of The Jonas of Amsterdam was captured on way home from Barbary and taken to England in 1591. [SPForeign.84.xliv]

WOLTERS, Mr, the British Agent at Rotterdam, in 1766. [TNA.HO pp.1766.148]

WOOD, JAMES, a seaman aboard the Rachel when bound from Newcastle for London, was captured by the Dutch on 24 July 1663 and imprisoned in Ostend. [Oostende] [SPDom.1663.688]

WOOD, THOMAS, born 1784, son of William Wood in Tetbury, Gloucestershire, died in Curacao on 13 October 1811. [GM.81.657]

WOOLLS, THOMAS A., married Miss Lewis from Jamaica, in Ostend on 4 May 1789. [GM.59.572]

WORSLEY, GEORGE HUGHES, minister of the Scots Church in Middelburg in Walcheren from 1759 to 1760, moved to London. [F.7.549]

WOTTON, ANNE, late wife of John Slater a gentleman in Bergen-op-Zoom, probate, 1620, PCC

WRIGHT, ISACKE, from Norwich, Norfolk, licensed to go to Leiden in Holland in 1637. [TNA]

WYBO, JOHN, born in Petham, Flanders, son of John Wybo, residing in Cornhill, London, probate, 1609, PCC

WYBO, PETER, of London and Flanders, probate, 1620, PCC

WYNDHAM, Sir THOMAS, in Bruges, [Brugge] probate, 1693, PCC

WYVILL, THOMAS, a gentleman from London, at Helvetsluis, probate, 1693, PCC

ANGLO-DUTCH LINKS, 1560-1860

SOME SHIPPING LINKS

Alexander, master Joseph Dodds, with four passengers, from Falmouth via Madeira bound for Surinam in in 1806 and in 1808. [ARM]

Coffee Planter, a galley, master John Graham, with one passenger, at Madeira in 1807 bound for Surinam. [ARM]
Commerce, master John Moncur, with three passengers, at Madeira in July 1807 bound for Demerara. [ARM]

Duckenfield, master William Dunbar, from London with sixteen passengers, at Madeira on 29 June 1807, bound for Surinam. [ARM]

Duke of Kent, master James Dougal, from Liverpool with two passengers, at Madeira on 22 March 1807 bound for Demerara. [ARM]

Earl Moira, master Robert Naylor, with five passengers, at Madeira in 1807, bound for Curacao. [ARM]

Enterprise, master William Burghes, with three passengers, at Madeira in 1806, bound for Surinam; master James Anderson, with twelve passengers, at Madeira in 1807 bound for Demerara. [ARM]

George, a galley, master James Pryce, from London via Madeira bound for Demerara in 1807. [ARM]

Good Intent, a brig, master Cornelius Stevens, at Madeira in July 1807 bound for Demerara. [ARM]

ANGLO-DUTCH LINKS, 1560-1860

Hopewell, a barque, master Lewis Hunt, arrived in Boston, Massachusetts, on 29 April 1712 from Surinam, with John Seylor a sailor. [NEHGS]

Hoxbury, a brig, master James Watson, with passengers, from Falmouth via Madeira bound for Demerara in 1808. [ARM.CM.Fun.600]

Howe, a brig, master John Lusk, from Falmouth via Madeira bound for Demerara, with five passengers in 1808. [ARM]

Indefatigable, master William Williamson, with two passengers, at Madeira on 21 July 1807 bound for Berbice. [ARM]

Katherine a brigantine, master John Breet, arrived in Boston, Massachusetts, on 7 April 1712 from Holland. [NEHGS]

Kingsmill, master John Barclay, with three passengers, at Madeira in July 1807, bound for Berbice. [ARM]

Mary and Anne, a brig, master John Watson, with seven passengers, from Falmouth via Madeira bound for Berbice in 1808. [ARM]

Mercury, a galley, master William Wemyss, with one passenger, at Madeira in July 1807, bound for Surinam. [ARM]

Nautilius, a brig, master Thomas Johnson, with four passengers, at Madeira in July 1807. [ARM]

Orange Tree of Amsterdam, 150 tons, at Plymouth bound for America in 1624. [ActsPC.V.448]

ANGLO-DUTCH LINKS, 1560-1860

Paxton, a brig, master Isaac Balston, from Falmouth with two passengers via Madeira bound for Demerara in 1808. [ARM]

Planet, master William Langley, from London with six passengers, via Madeira on 19 January 1807, bound for Demerara. [ARM]

Scipio, master William Briggs, from Falmouth via Madeira bound for Surinam in August 1806. [ARM]

Success, a ship, master William Thomas, arrived in Boston, Massachusetts, on 15 April 1712 from Surinam, with Johannes Van Harbergreen, a merchant. [NEHGS]

Surinam Galley, master John Hyndman, with four passengers, at Madeira in 1807 bound for Surinam. [ARM]

Swift, master Samuel Duett, with four passengers, at Madeira in July 1807 bound for Berbice. [ARM]

Trafalgar, a brig, master John Gibb, with two passengers, at Madeira in 1807, bound for Surinam. [ARM]

Tres Irmaos, master John McAuley, from London with six passengers, at Madeira on 15 July 1807 bound for Surinam. [ARM]

Tryall a sloop, master John Tuffton, arrived in Boston, Massachusetts, on 8 April 1712 from Surinam. [NEHGS]

Wilding, a galley, master Robert Freeman, from Portsmouth with eight passengers, at Madeira on 19 July 1807, bound for Demerara. [ARM]

www.ingramcontent.com/pod-product-compliance
Lightning Source LLC
Chambersburg PA
CBHW050842160426
43192CB00011B/2122